MW00958270

lift up your hearts

third edition

eucharistic prayers based on the *revised common lectionary*

year a

michael j. o'donnell, o.s.l.

OSL Publications

Ashland City TN

ISBN 978-1500810559

lift up your hearts
third edition
year a
Eucharistic Prayers Based on the *Revised Common Lectionary*

ISBN 978-1500810559

Produced and manufactured in the United States of America by
OSL Publications
The publishing ministry of the Order of Saint Luke
1002 Hunters Lane
Ashland City TN 37015

Colleen P. Gilrane, O. S. L., Editor

www. Saint-Luke.net

Acknowledgements: The basic form of The Great Thanksgiving is from *The United Methodist Hymnal: Book of United Methodist Worship* Service of Word and Table I (c)1972,1980,1985, 1989 The United Methodist Publishing House Used by permission.

Lectionary selections are from the *Revised Common Lectionary,* (c) 1992 Consultation on Common Texts. Used by permission.

Scripture quotations are from the *New Revised Standard Version Bible,* copyright 1989, Division of Christian Education of the National Council of the Churches of Christ in the United States of America. Used by permission. All rights reserved.

The Order of Saint Luke is a dispersed religious community, lay and clergy, male and female, dedicated to sacramental and liturgical scholarship, education and practice, and continuing spiritual formation. It is historically grounded in the Wesleyan tradition. Founded by Methodists, the Order also includes many persons in other Christian families.

The purpose of the publishing ministry is to put into the hands of students and practitioners resources which have theological, historical, ecumenical and practical integrity.

INTRODUCTION

The basic pattern for worship in the United Methodist Church is called Word and Table, and is found in T*he United Methodist Hymnal: Book of United Methodist Worship* (1988) (*UMH*) and *The United Methodist Book of Worship* (1992)*(BOW)*. The use of this pattern was reinforced in the document *This Holy Mystery,* adopted by the 2004 General Conference. (It is highly recommended that all leaders of Holy Communion read and become familiar with *This Holy Mystery*, which is available from the United Methodist General Board of Discipleship at http://www.gbod.org/worship/)

> Bishops, pastors, and congregations are expected to use the services of Word and Table in the official United Methodist hymnals and books of worship. Knowledgeable use of these resources allows for a balance of flexibility to meet contextual needs, and order that reflects our unity and connectional accountability.
>
> "An Order of Sunday Worship Using the Basic Pattern" (*UMH*; pages 3–5) offers flexibility for response to the activity of the Holy Spirit as well as the specifics of events and settings. In attending to the season, day, or occasion, presiders may insert words of their own composition or selections taken from fuller ritual texts as indicated in "A Service of Word and Table II" and "A Service of Word and Table III." (See *UMH*, "A Service of Word and Table II," pages 12–15; "A Service of Word and Table III," pages 15–16; musical settings, pages 17–25.)[1]

This instruction allows for flexibility within the framework of the basic pattern. The United Methodist approach to worship has been a blend of tradition and innovation. United Methodists have never been a people of one particular worship book. Local custom, rather than particular words, has been the primary criterion for putting together the weekly service. A pastor or worship committee can use this basic pattern with great flexibility making each service unique. It can address the needs of the people on that particular Sunday. Each week the common outline can be augmented with special prayers, anthems, hymns, scripture lessons and sermon.

Congregations that have been hearing the common lectionary as the primary beginning point for the service and sermon, have been enriched by hearing the full faith narrative over time. Conscientious worship planners work to tie the various parts of the service into a cohesive whole. However, for many congregations, there is a disconnect between Word and Table. When Holy Communion is just 'tacked on' at the end of the worship service with no regard to the scripture and theme for the day, the worshiper misses the fullness of the message.

This disconnection cheats us in our worship. If we are cheated, so much more so is God, who gave us both scripture and sacrament as means of grace. To divide them is to weaken each. It is unfortunate that until now the two evolutions in our worship—more frequent eucharist and use of a common lectionary—have not been coordinated to allow them to speak to and for each other.

---

[1] *This Holy Mystery: A United Methodist Understanding of Holy Communion*, General Board of Discipleship, Nashville, TN, 2003,2004, p. 24-25.

The complete pattern of Christian worship for the Lord's Day is Word and Table--the gospel is proclaimed in both Word and Sacrament. Word and Table are not in competition; rather they complement each other so as to constitute a whole service of worship. Their separation diminishes the fullness of life in the Spirit offered to us through faith in Jesus Christ.[2]

THE PURPOSE OF THIS BOOK

The eucharistic prayers (Great Thanksgivings) in this book are written for those pastors who are leading the people of God toward more frequent reception of the means of grace through the sacrament of Holy Communion and who follow the lections of the Revised Common Lectionary (1992). Prayers are included for all of the Sundays of the year, some Holy Days, and the days of Holy Week. The prayers follow the pattern of Word and Table II and III in *The United Methodist Hymnal: Book of United Methodist Worship*. Presiders who follow other patterns of eucharistic prayer will soon discover the flow of this form and will be able to adapt them easily.

The Great Thanksgiving is divided into three sections: Thanksgiving to the Father, *anamnesis* or Memorial to Jesus Christ, and *epiclesis* or Invocation of the Holy Spirit. A Service of Word and Table II (pp. 12-15, *UMH*) offers several places where the prayer can be altered to fit the current situation of the community; these are indicated by an asterisk (*). This book adds lectionary references in most of those places, as well as an expanded version of the "prayer after receiving" from Word and Table I for each celebration.

WHY A THIRD EDITION?

It has been fifteen years since the publication of *Lift Up Your Hearts (Revised and Expanded) Year A*. In many years of using these prayers, I have discovered that sometimes the words did not come as easily out of the mouth as they had into my mind and onto paper. I've also had multiple opportunities to reread the scripture lessons assigned by the lectionary, viewing those through liturgical eyes—trying to see what was sacramental in the texts that might not be obviously sacramental. As a result, this new edition has many new or rewritten prayers.

Each prayer now includes the Isaiah portion of the *anamnesis* that was left out of the earlier versions. I think that is a critical identification of who Jesus is to the world, then and now. The message foretold in Isaiah, as incarnated in Jesus, continues to be the message for us today, as does the incarnation itself. I think it's an essential piece, and I had left it out last time for practical reasons—it is not in Word and Table II which is the version I modified. I don't know if the original writers considered it to be of secondary importance, but I find it to be of primary importance. I took my cue from Word and Table II the first time, and said, "OK, this can be left out," but the more I've lived with the prayer over the years, the less comfortable I've been with that. What I have done for years now is reprint the prayer myself, even if I kept all the other words the same, and added the Isaiah prophecy to it. Now, it is built back in to each week's prayer.

---

[2] *This Holy Mystery*, p. 18.

You are encouraged to make your own modifications to the Prayers of Great Thanksgiving once you have prayed them enough that "they begin to pray you"[3]. Until that time, use this book as your resource.

USING *LIFT UP YOUR HEARTS* IN WORSHIP

Congregations with the *United Methodist Hymnal* may refer to the services of Word and Table II (pp. 12-15), Word and Table III (pp. 15-16), or the musical settings on pages 17 through 25 while a pastor reads from *Lift Up Your Hearts, 3rd Edition, Year C*, as the concluding words of each section that prompt the congregational responses are unchanged from the *Hymnal*. If this is the case, the prayers can be used as they appear in this book. All a pastor needs to do is print out the prayer assigned to a particular service, and insert the pages into a folder appropriate for use in worship[4]. The prayers are arranged in "sense lines," with line breaks put deliberately at sensible places to pause and breathe, to support readers.

Some pastors will wish to modify the prayers before using them. For example, in its section, "The Prayer of Great Thanksgiving," *This Holy Mystery* offers suggestions for greater spoken participation on the part of the people:

> The whole assembly might join in parts of the Great Thanksgiving that speak for them:
> (a) the memorial acclamation, beginning, "And so, in remembrance . . .";
> (b) an expression of intention to serve the world, beginning, "Make them be for us . . .";
> (c) the concluding doxology, beginning, "Through your Son Jesus Christ . . . ."

If you wish to make these modifications, you will need to do some preparation with your congregation so that they are ready. You might insert notes into the individual hymnals if you are using those, or you might copy and paste the prayers in this book into a word processor file and then make the relevant texts **bold** to indicate congregational speaking. *(More detailed instructions on how to copy text into a bulletin or other document can be found in the "read me" file on this CD.)* Some worship leaders may find useful the dismissals with blessing, ascriptions of glory, and versions of the Lord's Prayer that are included for reference at the end of the book, on pages 221 through 224.

May these prayers enrich your worship and your ministry. May they be a means of grace as you "lift up your hearts" to God in praise and prayer.

---

[3] Thanks to Dwight W. Vogel, OSL, for this phrase.

[4] Ceremonial binders, in colors of the liturgical seasons, are available from companies such as World Library Publications, Augsburg Fortress, Meyer•Vogelpohl and other sites you might find with an internet search.

NOTES FROM THE PUBLISHER:

To keep printing costs at a minimum, a decision was made to print the rubrics in these volumes in italicized print rather that the traditional red

If you wish to use these prayers at the altar, it is suggested that you go to your office supply store or local printer and have the spine removed and the pages either spiral-bound or drilled for use in a three-ring binder. Both should be available at a nominal cost and will allow the book to lay flat, allowing you full use of your hands.

You also have the option of purchasing Lift Up Your Hearts, Third Edition, on a disk containing pdf portfolios of all three years of the lectionary. You can print any of the prayers you wish to use from those pdf files. . The pdf files have the rubrics in red.

For more information, contact us at oslpublications@gmail.com.

Isaiah 2:1-5; Psalm 122; Romans 13:11-14; Matthew 24:36-44

The Lord be with you.
And also with you.
Lift up your hearts.
We lift them up to the Lord.
Let us give thanks to the Lord our God.
It is right to give our thanks and praise.

It is right, and a good and joyful thing
always and everywhere to give thanks to you,
Almighty God, Creator of heaven and earth.
You have established your house in the highest of places.
All the nations stream to it to learn of your ways;
the ways of peace and justice

And so, with your people on earth
and all the company of heaven,
we praise your name and join their unending hymn:

Holy, holy, holy Lord, God of power and might,
heaven and earth are full of your glory.
Hosanna in the highest.
Blessed is he who comes in the name of the Lord.
Hosanna in the highest.

Holy are you, and blessed is your Son Jesus Christ.
He is the way to you and
has taught us to be prepared for the day
when he comes in final victory.

Your Spirit anointed him
to preach good news to the poor,
to proclaim release to the captives and
recovering of sight to the blind,
to set at liberty those who are oppressed, and
to announce that the time had come
when you would save your people.
He healed the sick, fed the hungry, and ate with sinners.

By the baptism of his suffering, death, and resurrection,
  you gave birth to your church,
  delivered us from slavery to sin and death,
  and made with us a new covenant
  by water and the Spirit.

On the night in which he gave himself up for us
  he took bread, gave thanks to you, broke the bread,
  gave it to his disciples, and said,
"Take, eat; this is my body which is given for you.
Do this in remembrance of me."

When the supper was over he took the cup,
  gave thanks to you, gave it to his disciples, and said,
"Drink from this, all of you; this is my blood of the
  new covenant poured out for you and for many
    for the forgiveness of sins.
Do this as often as you drink it,
  in remembrance of me."

And so, in remembrance of these your mighty acts in Jesus Christ,
we offer ourselves in praise and thanksgiving
  as a holy and living sacrifice,
  in union with Christ's offering for us,
as we proclaim the mystery of faith.

Christ has died; Christ is risen; Christ will come again.

Pour out your Holy Spirit on us gathered here,
  and on these gifts of bread and wine.
Make them be for us the body and blood of Christ,
that we may be for the world the body of Christ,
  redeemed by his blood, that
  swords might be turned into plowshares and
    spears into pruning hooks, and
      there shall be peace for all humanity.

By your Spirit make us one with Christ,
    one with each other and
    one in ministry to all the world,
until Christ comes in final victory and
    we feast at the heavenly banquet.

Through your Son Jesus Christ,
with the Holy Spirit in your holy church,
all honor and glory is yours, almighty God,
    now and for ever.

Amen.

THE LORD'S PRAYER
And now with the confidence of children of God, let us pray: **Our Father…**

BREAKING THE BREAD
The pastor breaks the bread in silence, or while saying:
Because there is one loaf,
we, who are many, are one body, for we all partake of the one loaf.
The bread which we break is a sharing in the body of Christ.

The pastor lifts the cup in silence, or while saying:
The cup over which we give thanks is a sharing in the blood of Christ.

GIVING THE BREAD AND CUP
The bread and cup are given to the people, with these or other words being exchanged:
The body of Christ, given for you. **Amen.**
The blood of Christ, given for you. **Amen.**

PRAYER AFTER RECEIVING
Eternal God, we give you thanks for this holy mystery
    in which you have given yourself to us.
May it strengthen us to be instruments of your peace.
Grant that we may go into the world
    in the strength of your Spirit,
    to give ourselves for others.
in the name of Jesus Christ our Lord.
Amen.

Second Sunday of Advent (a)

Isaiah 11:1-10; Psalm 72:1-7, 18-19; Romans 15:4-13; Matthew 3:1-12

The Lord be with you.
And also with you.
Lift up your hearts.
We lift them up to the Lord.
Let us give thanks to the Lord our God.
It is right to give our thanks and praise.

It is right, and a good and joyful thing
    always and everywhere to give thanks to you,
        Almighty God, Creator of heaven and earth.
You brought forth a shoot from the stump of Jesse.
Your spirit rested upon him;
    the spirit of wisdom and understanding,
        of counsel and might.
This root of Jesse stands as a signal to all the peoples,
    all the nations of the world.

And so, with your people on earth
    and all the company of heaven,
    we praise your name and join their unending hymn:

Holy, holy, holy Lord, God of power and might,
heaven and earth are full of your glory.
    Hosanna in the highest.
Blessed is he who comes in the name of the Lord.
    Hosanna in the highest.

Holy are you, and blessed is your Son Jesus Christ.
He is that very shoot of Jesse,
  the promise revealed, the hope fulfilled.
Your Spirit anointed him
    to preach good news to the poor,
    to proclaim release to the captives and
    recovering of sight to the blind,
    to set at liberty those who are oppressed, and
    to announce that the time had come
    when you would save your people.
He healed the sick, fed the hungry, and ate with sinners.

By the baptism of his suffering, death, and resurrection,
   you gave birth to your church,
   delivered us from slavery to sin and death,
   and made with us a new covenant
   by water and the Spirit.

On the night in which he gave himself up for us
   he took bread, gave thanks to you, broke the bread,
   gave it to his disciples, and said,
"Take, eat; this is my body which is given for you.
Do this in remembrance of me."

When the supper was over he took the cup,
   gave thanks to you, gave it to his disciples, and said,
"Drink from this, all of you; this is my blood of the
   new covenant poured out for you and for many
      for the forgiveness of sins.
Do this as often as you drink it,
   in remembrance of me."

And so, in remembrance of these your mighty acts in Jesus Christ,
we offer ourselves in praise and thanksgiving
   as a holy and living sacrifice,
   in union with Christ's offering for us,
as we proclaim the mystery of faith.

Christ has died; Christ is risen; Christ will come again.

Pour out your Holy Spirit on us gathered here,
   and on these gifts of bread and wine.
Make them be for us the body and blood of Christ,
that we may be for the world the body of Christ,
   redeemed by his blood, that
      all might live in peace and harmony and
      together give glory to you, O Lord.

By your Spirit make us one with Christ,
   one with each other and
   one in ministry to all the world,
until Christ comes in final victory and
   we feast at the heavenly banquet.

Through your Son Jesus Christ,
with the Holy Spirit in your holy church,
all honor and glory is yours, almighty God,
    now and for ever.

Amen.

THE LORD'S PRAYER

And now with the confidence of children of God, let us pray: **Our Father...**

BREAKING THE BREAD

The pastor breaks the bread in silence, or while saying:
Because there is one loaf,
we, who are many, are one body, for we all partake of the one loaf.
The bread which we break is a sharing in the body of Christ.

The pastor lifts the cup in silence, or while saying:
The cup over which we give thanks is a sharing in the blood of Christ.

GIVING THE BREAD AND CUP

The bread and cup are given to the people, with these or other words being exchanged:
The body of Christ, given for you. **Amen.**
The blood of Christ, given for you. **Amen.**

PRAYER AFTER RECEIVING

Eternal God, we give you thanks for this holy mystery
    in which you have given yourself to us.
Open the hearts of the world to the joy of this gift of Jesus Christ
    that all might know and believe.
Grant that we may go into the world
    in the strength of your Spirit,
        to give ourselves for others.
in the name of Jesus Christ our Lord.
Amen.

NOTE: Benedictions based on Romans 15 (see page 223) are especially
    appropriate this Sunday.

Third Sunday of Advent (a)

Isaiah 35:1-10; Psalm 146:5-10 or Luke 1:47-55; James 5:7-10; Matthew 11:2-11

The Lord be with you.
And also with you.
Lift up your hearts.
We lift them up to the Lord.
Let us give thanks to the Lord our God.
It is right to give our thanks and praise.

It is right, and a good and joyful thing
    always and everywhere to give thanks to you,
    Almighty God, Creator of heaven and earth.
Our souls magnify you oh Lord,
  our spirits rejoice in you our Savior.
You have done great things for us,
  and holy is your name.
And so, with your people on earth
    and all the company of heaven,
    we praise your name and join their unending hymn:

Holy, holy, holy Lord, God of power and might,
heaven and earth are full of your glory.
    Hosanna in the highest.
Blessed is he who comes in the name of the Lord.
    Hosanna in the highest.

Holy are you, and blessed is your Son Jesus Christ.
Through him, you have brought down the powerful
    from their thrones,
    and lifted up the lowly.

Your Spirit anointed him
    to preach good news to the poor,
    to proclaim release to the captives and
    recovering of sight to the blind,
    to set at liberty those who are oppressed, and
    to announce that the time had come
    when you would save your people.
He healed the sick, fed the hungry, and ate with sinners.

By the baptism of his suffering, death, and resurrection,
you gave birth to your church,
delivered us from slavery to sin and death,
and made with us a new covenant
by water and the Spirit.

On the night in which he gave himself up for us
he took bread, gave thanks to you, broke the bread,
gave it to his disciples, and said,
"Take, eat; this is my body which is given for you.
Do this in remembrance of me."

When the supper was over he took the cup,
gave thanks to you, gave it to his disciples, and said,
"Drink from this, all of you; this is my blood of the
new covenant poured out for you and for many
for the forgiveness of sins.
Do this as often as you drink it,
in remembrance of me."

And so, in remembrance of these your mighty acts in Jesus Christ,
we offer ourselves in praise and thanksgiving
as a holy and living sacrifice,
in union with Christ's offering for us,
as we proclaim the mystery of faith.

Christ has died; Christ is risen; Christ will come again.

Pour out your Holy Spirit on us gathered here,
and on these gifts of bread and wine.
Make them be for us the body and blood of Christ,
that we may be for the world the body of Christ,
redeemed by his blood,
that we might be patient for the coming of the Lord.

By your Spirit make us one with Christ,
one with each other and
one in ministry to all the world,
until Christ comes in final victory and
we feast at the heavenly banquet.

Through your Son Jesus Christ,
with the Holy Spirit in your holy church,
all honor and glory is yours, almighty God,
    now and for ever.
Amen.

THE LORD'S PRAYER

And now with the confidence of children of God, let us pray: **Our Father...**

BREAKING THE BREAD

The pastor breaks the bread in silence, or while saying:
Because there is one loaf,
we, who are many, are one body, for we all partake of the one loaf.
The bread which we break is a sharing in the body of Christ.

The pastor lifts the cup in silence, or while saying:
The cup over which we give thanks is a sharing in the blood of Christ.

GIVING THE BREAD AND CUP

The bread and cup are given to the people, with these or other words being exchanged:
The body of Christ, given for you. **Amen.**
The blood of Christ, given for you. **Amen.**

PRAYER AFTER RECEIVING

Eternal God, we give you thanks for this holy mystery
    in which you have given yourself to us.
Make us examples of suffering and patience
    for the sake of the gospel.
Grant that we may go into the world
    in the strength of your Spirit,
    to give ourselves for others.
in the name of Jesus Christ our Lord.
Amen.

*NOTE: Benediction based on James 5:7-9 (see page 223) is especially appropriate
    this Sunday.*

Fourth Sunday of Advent (a)

Isaiah 7:10-16; Psalm 80:1-7, 17-19; Romans 1:1-7; Matthew 1:18-25

The Lord be with you.
And also with you.
Lift up your hearts.
We lift them up to the Lord.
Let us give thanks to the Lord our God.
It is right to give our thanks and praise.

It is right, and a good and joyful thing
    always and everywhere to give thanks to you,
    Almighty God, Creator of heaven and earth.
You chose Mary the virgin to bear your son,
    that you might be present with us
    and that we might know you.

And so, with your people on earth
    and all the company of heaven,
    we praise your name and join their unending hymn:

Holy, holy, holy Lord, God of power and might,
heaven and earth are full of your glory.
    Hosanna in the highest.
Blessed is he who comes in the name of the Lord.
    Hosanna in the highest.

Holy are you, and blessed is your Son Jesus Christ.
Conceived by your Spirit and born of Mary
    he is truly Emmanuel, God-with-us.

Your Spirit anointed him
    to preach good news to the poor,
    to proclaim release to the captives and
    recovering of sight to the blind,
    to set at liberty those who are oppressed, and
    to announce that the time had come
    when you would save your people.
He healed the sick, fed the hungry, and ate with sinners.

By the baptism of his suffering, death, and resurrection,
    you gave birth to your church,
    delivered us from slavery to sin and death,
    and made with us a new covenant
    by water and the Spirit.

On the night in which he gave himself up for us
    he took bread, gave thanks to you, broke the bread,
    gave it to his disciples, and said,
"Take, eat; this is my body which is given for you.
Do this in remembrance of me."

When the supper was over he took the cup,
    gave thanks to you, gave it to his disciples, and said,
"Drink from this, all of you; this is my blood of the
    new covenant poured out for you and for many
        for the forgiveness of sins.
Do this as often as you drink it,
    in remembrance of me."

And so, in remembrance of these your mighty acts in Jesus Christ,
we offer ourselves in praise and thanksgiving
    as a holy and living sacrifice,
    in union with Christ's offering for us,
as we proclaim the mystery of faith.

Christ has died; Christ is risen; Christ will come again.

Pour out your Holy Spirit on us gathered here,
    and on these gifts of bread and wine.
Make them be for us the body and blood of Christ,
that we may be for the world the body of Christ,
    redeemed by his blood,
for we are called to be saints and
    bring the world to Christ.

By your Spirit make us one with Christ,
    one with each other and
    one in ministry to all the world,
until Christ comes in final victory and
    we feast at the heavenly banquet.

Through your Son Jesus Christ,
with the Holy Spirit in your holy church,
all honor and glory is yours, almighty God,
    now and for ever.

Amen.

THE LORD'S PRAYER

And now with the confidence of children of God, let us pray: **Our Father...**

BREAKING THE BREAD

The pastor breaks the bread in silence, or while saying:
Because there is one loaf,
we, who are many, are one body, for we all partake of the one loaf.
The bread which we break is a sharing in the body of Christ.

The pastor lifts the cup in silence, or while saying:
The cup over which we give thanks is a sharing in the blood of Christ.

GIVING THE BREAD AND CUP

The bread and cup are given to the people, with these or other words being exchanged:
The body of Christ, given for you. **Amen.**
The blood of Christ, given for you. **Amen.**

PRAYER AFTER RECEIVING

Eternal God, we give you thanks for this holy mystery
    in which you have given yourself to us.
Fulfill in us your desire for all humanity.
Grant that we may go into the world
    in the strength of your Spirit,
        to give ourselves for others.
in the name of Jesus Christ our Lord.
Amen.

Christmas Eve & Day (proper 1)

Isaiah 9:2-7; Psalm 96; Titus 2:11-14; Luke 2:1-14, (15-20)

The Lord be with you.
And also with you.
Lift up your hearts.
We lift them up to the Lord.
Let us give thanks to the Lord our God.
It is right to give our thanks and praise.

It is right, and a good and joyful thing
    always and everywhere to give thanks to you,
      Almighty God, Creator of heaven and earth.
Your people who walked in darkness have seen a great light;
    those who dwelt in a land of deep darkness, on them has light shined.
You have multiplied the nation; you have increased its joy.

And so, with your people on earth
    and all the company of heaven,
      we praise your name and join their unending hymn:

Holy, holy, holy Lord, God of power and might,
heaven and earth are full of your glory.
    Hosanna in the highest.
Blessed is he who comes in the name of the Lord.
    Hosanna in the highest.

Holy are you, and blessed is your Son Jesus Christ.
We rejoice as your people, for to us a child is born, to us a son is given;
and the government shall be upon his shoulder.
His name shall be called Wonderful Counselor,
    Mighty God, Everlasting Father, Prince of Peace.

Your Spirit anointed him
    to preach good news to the poor,
    to proclaim release to the captives and
    recovering of sight to the blind,
    to set at liberty those who are oppressed, and
    to announce that the time had come
    when you would save your people.
He healed the sick, fed the hungry, and ate with sinners.

By the baptism of his suffering, death, and resurrection,
    you gave birth to your church,
    delivered us from slavery to sin and death,
    and made with us a new covenant
    by water and the Spirit.

On the night in which he gave himself up for us
    he took bread, gave thanks to you, broke the bread,
    gave it to his disciples, and said,
"Take, eat; this is my body which is given for you.
Do this in remembrance of me."

When the supper was over he took the cup,
    gave thanks to you, gave it to his disciples, and said,
"Drink from this, all of you; this is my blood of the
    new covenant poured out for you and for many
        for the forgiveness of sins.
Do this as often as you drink it,
    in remembrance of me."

And so, in remembrance of these your mighty acts in Jesus Christ,
we offer ourselves in praise and thanksgiving
    as a holy and living sacrifice,
    in union with Christ's offering for us,
as we proclaim the mystery of faith.

Christ has died; Christ is risen; Christ will come again.

Pour out your Holy Spirit on us gathered here,
    and on these gifts of bread and wine.
Make them be for us the body and blood of Christ,
that we may be for the world the body of Christ,
    redeemed by his blood,
that we might bring to all the people
    the good news of great joy,
that the grace of God has appeared,
    bringing salvation to all.

By your Spirit make us one with Christ,
   one with each other and
   one in ministry to all the world,
until Christ comes in final victory and
   we feast at the heavenly banquet.

Through your Son Jesus Christ,
with the Holy Spirit in your holy church,
all honor and glory is yours, almighty God,
   now and for ever.

Amen.

THE LORD'S PRAYER
And now with the confidence of children of God, let us pray: **Our Father…**

BREAKING THE BREAD
The pastor breaks the bread in silence, or while saying:
Because there is one loaf,
we, who are many, are one body, for we all partake of the one loaf.
The bread which we break is a sharing in the body of Christ.

The pastor lifts the cup in silence, or while saying:
The cup over which we give thanks is a sharing in the blood of Christ.

GIVING THE BREAD AND CUP
The bread and cup are given to the people, with these or other words being exchanged:
The body of Christ, given for you. **Amen.**
The blood of Christ, given for you. **Amen.**

PRAYER AFTER RECEIVING
Eternal God, we give you thanks for this holy mystery
   in which you have given yourself to us.
Through it we proclaim the blessed hope—
   the appearing of our great God and Savior Jesus Christ.
Grant that we may go into the world
      in the strength of your Spirit,
      to give ourselves for others.
in the name of Jesus Christ our Lord.
Amen.

Christmas Eve & Day (proper 2)

Isaiah 62:6-12; Psalm 97; Titus 3:4-7; Luke 2 (1-7), 8-20

The Lord be with you.
And also with you.
Lift up your hearts.
We lift them up to the Lord.
Let us give thanks to the Lord our God.
It is right to give our thanks and praise.

It is right, and a good and joyful thing
    always and everywhere to give thanks to you,
      Almighty God, Creator of heaven and earth.
You are the Lord, our king!
Let the world rejoice; let the many coastlands be glad!
The heavens proclaim your righteousness;
    and all the peoples behold your glory.

And so, with your people on earth
    and all the company of heaven,
      we praise your name and join their unending hymn:

Holy, holy, holy Lord, God of power and might,
heaven and earth are full of your glory.
    Hosanna in the highest.
Blessed is he who comes in the name of the Lord.
    Hosanna in the highest.

Holy are you, and blessed is your Son Jesus Christ.
who was born to us this day in the city of David,
    our savior, who is Christ the Lord.

Your Spirit anointed him
    to preach good news to the poor,
    to proclaim release to the captives and
    recovering of sight to the blind,
    to set at liberty those who are oppressed, and
    to announce that the time had come
    when you would save your people.
He healed the sick, fed the hungry, and ate with sinners.

By the baptism of his suffering, death, and resurrection,
   you gave birth to your church,
   delivered us from slavery to sin and death,
   and made with us a new covenant
   by water and the Spirit.

On the night in which he gave himself up for us
   he took bread, gave thanks to you, broke the bread,
   gave it to his disciples, and said,
"Take, eat; this is my body which is given for you.
Do this in remembrance of me."

When the supper was over he took the cup,
   gave thanks to you, gave it to his disciples, and said,
"Drink from this, all of you; this is my blood of the
   new covenant poured out for you and for many
      for the forgiveness of sins.
Do this as often as you drink it,
   in remembrance of me."

And so, in remembrance of these your mighty acts in Jesus Christ,
we offer ourselves in praise and thanksgiving
   as a holy and living sacrifice,
   in union with Christ's offering for us,
as we proclaim the mystery of faith.

Christ has died; Christ is risen; Christ will come again.

Pour out your Holy Spirit on us gathered here,
   and on these gifts of bread and wine.
Make them be for us the body and blood of Christ,
that we may be for the world the body of Christ,
   redeemed by his blood,
so that having been justified by his grace,
   we might become heirs according to the hope of eternal life.

By your Spirit make us one with Christ,
   one with each other and
   one in ministry to all the world,
until Christ comes in final victory and
   we feast at the heavenly banquet.

Through your Son Jesus Christ,
with the Holy Spirit in your holy church,
all honor and glory is yours, almighty God,
    now and for ever.

Amen.

THE LORD'S PRAYER

And now with the confidence of children of God, let us pray: **Our Father...**

BREAKING THE BREAD

The pastor breaks the bread in silence, or while saying:
Because there is one loaf,
we, who are many, are one body, for we all partake of the one loaf.
The bread which we break is a sharing in the body of Christ.

The pastor lifts the cup in silence, or while saying:
The cup over which we give thanks is a sharing in the blood of Christ.

GIVING THE BREAD AND CUP

The bread and cup are given to the people, with these or other words being exchanged:
The body of Christ, given for you. **Amen.**
The blood of Christ, given for you. **Amen.**

PRAYER AFTER RECEIVING

Eternal God, we give you thanks for this holy mystery
    in which you have given yourself to us.
You have saved us by your mercy and poured out your Spirit upon us.
Grant that we may go into the world
    in the strength of your Spirit,
    to give ourselves for others.
in the name of Jesus Christ our Lord.
Amen.

Christmas Eve & Day (proper 3)

Isaiah 52:7-10; Psalm 98; Hebrews 1:1-4, (5-12); John 1:1-14

The Lord be with you.
And also with you.
Lift up your hearts.
We lift them up to the Lord.
Let us give thanks to the Lord our God.
It is right to give our thanks and praise.

It is right, and a good and joyful thing
    always and everywhere to give thanks to you,
    Almighty God, Creator of heaven and earth.
We sing with joy a new song
for you have redeemed your people.
You have bared your holy arm before the nations.

Your salvation shall be made known to the ends of the earth.
And so, with your people on earth
    and all the company of heaven,
    we praise your name and join their unending hymn:

Holy, holy, holy Lord, God of power and might,
heaven and earth are full of your glory.
    Hosanna in the highest.
Blessed is he who comes in the name of the Lord.
    Hosanna in the highest.

Holy are you, and blessed is your Son Jesus Christ.
He was with you in the beginning; the Word made flesh.
All things have come into being through him.
In him was life, and the life was the light of all people.

Your Spirit anointed him
    to preach good news to the poor,
    to proclaim release to the captives and
    recovering of sight to the blind,
    to set at liberty those who are oppressed, and
    to announce that the time had come
    when you would save your people.
He healed the sick, fed the hungry, and ate with sinners.

By the baptism of his suffering, death, and resurrection,
   you gave birth to your church,
   delivered us from slavery to sin and death,
   and made with us a new covenant
   by water and the Spirit.

On the night in which he gave himself up for us
   he took bread, gave thanks to you, broke the bread,
   gave it to his disciples, and said,
"Take, eat; this is my body which is given for you.
Do this in remembrance of me."

When the supper was over he took the cup,
   gave thanks to you, gave it to his disciples, and said,
"Drink from this, all of you; this is my blood of the
   new covenant poured out for you and for many
      for the forgiveness of sins.
Do this as often as you drink it,
   in remembrance of me."

And so, in remembrance of these your mighty acts in Jesus Christ,
we offer ourselves in praise and thanksgiving
   as a holy and living sacrifice,
   in union with Christ's offering for us,
as we proclaim the mystery of faith.

Christ has died; Christ is risen; Christ will come again.

Pour out your Holy Spirit on us gathered here,
   and on these gifts of bread and wine.
Make them be for us the body and blood of Christ,
that we may be for the world the body of Christ,
   redeemed by his blood,
 through which we have been given the power to become children of God.

By your Spirit make us one with Christ,
   one with each other and
   one in ministry to all the world,
until Christ comes in final victory and
   we feast at the heavenly banquet.

Through your Son Jesus Christ,
with the Holy Spirit in your holy church,
all honor and glory is yours, almighty God,
    now and for ever.

Amen.

THE LORD'S PRAYER
And now with the confidence of children of God, let us pray: **Our Father...**

BREAKING THE BREAD
The pastor breaks the bread in silence, or while saying:
Because there is one loaf,
we, who are many, are one body, for we all partake of the one loaf.
The bread which we break is a sharing in the body of Christ.

The pastor lifts the cup in silence, or while saying:
The cup over which we give thanks is a sharing in the blood of Christ.

GIVING THE BREAD AND CUP
The bread and cup are given to the people, with these or other words being exchanged:
The body of Christ, given for you. **Amen.**
The blood of Christ, given for you. **Amen.**

PRAYER AFTER RECEIVING
Eternal God, we give you thanks for this holy mystery
    in which you have given yourself to us.
Through it may we shed Christ's light that overcomes the darkness.
Grant that we may go into the world
    in the strength of your Spirit,
        to give ourselves for others.
in the name of Jesus Christ our Lord.
Amen.

First Sunday After Christmas Day (a)

Isaiah 63:7-9; Psalm 148; Hebrews 2:10-18; Matthew 2:13-23

The Lord be with you.
And also with you.
Lift up your hearts.
We lift them up to the Lord.
Let us give thanks to the Lord our God.
It is right to give our thanks and praise.

It is right, and a good and joyful thing
    always and everywhere to give thanks to you,
    Almighty God, Creator of heaven and earth.
According to your mercy and steadfast love,
    you sent a savior to your people
        to lift them up and carry them.

And so, with your people on earth
    and all the company of heaven,
    we praise your name and join their unending hymn:

Holy, holy, holy Lord, God of power and might,
heaven and earth are full of your glory.
    Hosanna in the highest.
Blessed is he who comes in the name of the Lord.
    Hosanna in the highest.

Holy are you, and blessed is your Son Jesus Christ.
He became like us in every respect,
    so that he might be
        a merciful and faithful high priest in your service,
        and a sacrifice of atonement for the sins of the people.

Your Spirit anointed him
    to preach good news to the poor,
    to proclaim release to the captives and
    recovering of sight to the blind,
    to set at liberty those who are oppressed, and
    to announce that the time had come
    when you would save your people.
He healed the sick, fed the hungry, and ate with sinners.

By the baptism of his suffering, death, and resurrection,
    you gave birth to your church,
    delivered us from slavery to sin and death,
    and made with us a new covenant
    by water and the Spirit.

On the night in which he gave himself up for us
    he took bread, gave thanks to you, broke the bread,
    gave it to his disciples, and said,
"Take, eat; this is my body which is given for you.
Do this in remembrance of me."

When the supper was over he took the cup,
    gave thanks to you, gave it to his disciples, and said,
"Drink from this, all of you; this is my blood of the
    new covenant poured out for you and for many
        for the forgiveness of sins.
Do this as often as you drink it,
    in remembrance of me."

And so, in remembrance of these your mighty acts in Jesus Christ,
we offer ourselves in praise and thanksgiving
    as a holy and living sacrifice,
    in union with Christ's offering for us,
as we proclaim the mystery of faith.

Christ has died; Christ is risen; Christ will come again.

Pour out your Holy Spirit on us gathered here,
    and on these gifts of bread and wine.
Make them be for us the body and blood of Christ,
that we may be for the world the body of Christ,
    redeemed by his blood,
        through which we are lifted up and carried.

By your Spirit make us one with Christ,
    one with each other and
    one in ministry to all the world,
until Christ comes in final victory and
    we feast at the heavenly banquet.

Through your Son Jesus Christ,
with the Holy Spirit in your holy church,
all honor and glory is yours, almighty God,
    now and for ever.

Amen.

THE LORD'S PRAYER

And now with the confidence of children of God, let us pray: **Our Father...**

BREAKING THE BREAD

The pastor breaks the bread in silence, or while saying:
Because there is one loaf,
we, who are many, are one body, for we all partake of the one loaf.
The bread which we break is a sharing in the body of Christ.

The pastor lifts the cup in silence, or while saying:
The cup over which we give thanks is a sharing in the blood of Christ.

GIVING THE BREAD AND CUP

The bread and cup are given to the people, with these or other words being exchanged:
The body of Christ, given for you. **Amen.**
The blood of Christ, given for you. **Amen.**

PRAYER AFTER RECEIVING

Eternal God, we give you thanks for this holy mystery
    in which you have given yourself to us.
May we be a helping hand to all in need.
Grant that we may go into the world
    in the strength of your Spirit,
        to give ourselves for others.
in the name of Jesus Christ our Lord.
Amen.

Second Sunday After Christmas Day (a)

Jeremiah 31:7-14; Psalm 147:12-20; Ephesians 1:3-14; John 1:(1-9) 10-18

The Lord be with you.
And also with you.
Lift up your hearts.
We lift them up to the Lord.
Let us give thanks to the Lord our God.
It is right to give our thanks and praise.

It is right, and a good and joyful thing
    always and everywhere to give thanks to you,
    Almighty God, Creator of heaven and earth.
You were in the beginning; you are the Word.
All things come into being through you
    and without you not one thing is made.

And so, with your people on earth
    and all the company of heaven,
    we praise your name and join their unending hymn:

Holy, holy, holy Lord, God of power and might,
heaven and earth are full of your glory.
    Hosanna in the highest.
Blessed is he who comes in the name of the Lord.
    Hosanna in the highest.

Holy are you, and blessed is your Son Jesus Christ.
He was in the beginning with you.
He is the Word made flesh to dwell among us
    and lead us to you.

Your Spirit anointed him
    to preach good news to the poor,
    to proclaim release to the captives and
    recovering of sight to the blind,
    to set at liberty those who are oppressed, and
    to announce that the time had come
    when you would save your people.
He healed the sick, fed the hungry, and ate with sinners.

By the baptism of his suffering, death, and resurrection,
    you gave birth to your church,
    delivered us from slavery to sin and death,
     and made with us a new covenant
    by water and the Spirit.

On the night in which he gave himself up for us
    he took bread, gave thanks to you, broke the bread,
    gave it to his disciples, and said,
"Take, eat; this is my body which is given for you.
Do this in remembrance of me."

When the supper was over he took the cup,
    gave thanks to you, gave it to his disciples, and said,
"Drink from this, all of you; this is my blood of the
    new covenant poured out for you and for many
        for the forgiveness of sins.
Do this as often as you drink it,
    in remembrance of me."

And so, in remembrance of these your mighty acts in Jesus Christ,
we offer ourselves in praise and thanksgiving
    as a holy and living sacrifice,
    in union with Christ's offering for us,
as we proclaim the mystery of faith.

Christ has died; Christ is risen; Christ will come again.

Pour out your Holy Spirit on us gathered here,
    and on these gifts of bread and wine.
Make them be for us the body and blood of Christ,
that we may be for the world the body of Christ,
    redeemed by his blood,
        for he is the light that enlightens us.

By your Spirit make us one with Christ,
    one with each other and
    one in ministry to all the world,
until Christ comes in final victory and
    we feast at the heavenly banquet.

Through your Son Jesus Christ,
with the Holy Spirit in your holy church,
all honor and glory is yours, almighty God,
    now and for ever.
Amen.

THE LORD'S PRAYER

And now with the confidence of children of God, let us pray: **Our Father…**

BREAKING THE BREAD

The pastor breaks the bread in silence, or while saying:
Because there is one loaf,
we, who are many, are one body, for we all partake of the one loaf.
The bread which we break is a sharing in the body of Christ.

The pastor lifts the cup in silence, or while saying:
The cup over which we give thanks is a sharing in the blood of Christ.

GIVING THE BREAD AND CUP

The bread and cup are given to the people, with these or other words being exchanged:
The body of Christ, given for you. **Amen.**
The blood of Christ, given for you. **Amen.**

PRAYER AFTER RECEIVING

Eternal God, we give you thanks for this holy mystery
    in which you have given yourself to us.
Through it we receive the fullness of your grace and mercy.
Grant that we may go into the world
    in the strength of your Spirit,
        to give ourselves for others.
in the name of Jesus Christ our Lord.
Amen.

The Holy Name of Jesus [January 1]

Numbers 6:22-27; Psalm 8; Galatians 4:4-7 or Philippians 2:5-11; Luke 2:15-21

The Lord be with you.
And also with you.
Lift up your hearts.
We lift them up to the Lord.
Let us give thanks to the Lord our God.
It is right to give our thanks and praise.

It is right, and a good and joyful thing
    always and everywhere to give thanks to you,
    Almighty God, Creator of heaven and earth.
We look at your heavens, the work of your fingers,
    the moon and the stars that you have established;
    what are human beings that you are mindful of us, mortals that you care for us?
Yet you have made us a little lower than yourself,
    and crowned us with glory and honor.

And so, with your people on earth
    and all the company of heaven,
    we praise your name and join their unending hymn:

Holy, holy, holy Lord, God of power and might,
heaven and earth are full of your glory.
    Hosanna in the highest.
Blessed is he who comes in the name of the Lord.
    Hosanna in the highest.

Holy are you, and blessed is your Son Jesus Christ.
At his name every knee shall bow
    and every tongue confess that Jesus Christ is Lord.

Your Spirit anointed him
    to preach good news to the poor,
    to proclaim release to the captives and
    recovering of sight to the blind,
    to set at liberty those who are oppressed, and
    to announce that the time had come
    when you would save your people.
He healed the sick, fed the hungry, and ate with sinners.

By the baptism of his suffering, death, and resurrection,
    you gave birth to your church,
    delivered us from slavery to sin and death,
    and made with us a new covenant
    by water and the Spirit.

On the night in which he gave himself up for us
    he took bread, gave thanks to you, broke the bread,
    gave it to his disciples, and said,
"Take, eat; this is my body which is given for you.
Do this in remembrance of me."

When the supper was over he took the cup,
    gave thanks to you, gave it to his disciples, and said,
"Drink from this, all of you; this is my blood of the
    new covenant poured out for you and for many
        for the forgiveness of sins.
Do this as often as you drink it,
    in remembrance of me."

And so, in remembrance of these your mighty acts in Jesus Christ,
we offer ourselves in praise and thanksgiving
    as a holy and living sacrifice,
    in union with Christ's offering for us,
as we proclaim the mystery of faith.

Christ has died; Christ is risen; Christ will come again.

Pour out your Holy Spirit on us gathered here,
    and on these gifts of bread and wine.
Make them be for us the body and blood of Christ,
that we may be for the world the body of Christ,
    redeemed by his blood
that in our hearts and with our tongues we might cry," Abba! Father!"

By your Spirit make us one with Christ,
    one with each other and
    one in ministry to all the world,
until Christ comes in final victory and
    we feast at the heavenly banquet.

Through your Son Jesus Christ,
with the Holy Spirit in your holy church,
all honor and glory is yours, almighty God,
    now and for ever.

Amen.

THE LORD'S PRAYER

And now with the confidence of children of God, let us pray: **Our Father...**

BREAKING THE BREAD

The pastor breaks the bread in silence, or while saying:
Because there is one loaf,
we, who are many, are one body, for we all partake of the one loaf.
The bread which we break is a sharing in the body of Christ.

The pastor lifts the cup in silence, or while saying:
The cup over which we give thanks is a sharing in the blood of Christ.

GIVING THE BREAD AND CUP

The bread and cup are given to the people, with these or other words being exchanged:
The body of Christ, given for you. **Amen.**
The blood of Christ, given for you. **Amen.**

PRAYER AFTER RECEIVING

Eternal God, we give you thanks for this holy mystery
    in which you have given yourself to us.
In the power of the holy name of Jesus,
    grant that we may go into the world
    in the strength of your Spirit,
    to give ourselves for others.
in the name of Jesus Christ our Lord.
Amen.

Note: The text from Numbers is a traditional benediction—see page 214

New Year's Day

Ecclesiastes 3:1-13; Psalm 8; Revelation 21:1-6a; Matthew 25:31-46

The Lord be with you.
And also with you.
Lift up your hearts.
We lift them up to the Lord.
Let us give thanks to the Lord our God.
It is right to give our thanks and praise.

It is right, and a good and joyful thing
    always and everywhere to give thanks to you,
    Almighty God, Creator of heaven and earth.
You made all things and called them good.
You have given a season for everything
    and a time of renewal and recommitment.

And so, with your people on earth
    and all the company of heaven,
    we praise your name and join their unending hymn:

Holy, holy, holy Lord, God of power and might,
heaven and earth are full of your glory.
    Hosanna in the highest.
Blessed is he who comes in the name of the Lord.
    Hosanna in the highest.

Holy are you, and blessed is your Son Jesus Christ.
Who lived and taught a life of compassion and
    compels us to follow his ways.

Your Spirit anointed him
    to preach good news to the poor,
    to proclaim release to the captives and
    recovering of sight to the blind,
    to set at liberty those who are oppressed, and
    to announce that the time had come
    when you would save your people.
He healed the sick, fed the hungry, and ate with sinners.

By the baptism of his suffering, death, and resurrection,
    you gave birth to your church,
    delivered us from slavery to sin and death,
    and made with us a new covenant
    by water and the Spirit.

On the night in which he gave himself up for us
    he took bread, gave thanks to you, broke the bread,
    gave it to his disciples, and said,
"Take, eat; this is my body which is given for you.
Do this in remembrance of me."

When the supper was over he took the cup,
    gave thanks to you, gave it to his disciples, and said,
"Drink from this, all of you; this is my blood of the
    new covenant poured out for you and for many
        for the forgiveness of sins.
Do this as often as you drink it,
    in remembrance of me."

And so, in remembrance of these your mighty acts in Jesus Christ,
we offer ourselves in praise and thanksgiving
    as a holy and living sacrifice,
    in union with Christ's offering for us,
as we proclaim the mystery of faith.

Christ has died; Christ is risen; Christ will come again.

Pour out your Holy Spirit on us gathered here,
    and on these gifts of bread and wine.
Make them be for us the body and blood of Christ,
that we may be for the world the body of Christ,
    redeemed by his blood,
for you have promised a new order
    in which all tears will be wiped away and death shall be no more.

By your Spirit make us one with Christ,
    one with each other and
    one in ministry to all the world,
until Christ comes in final victory and
    we feast at the heavenly banquet.

Through your Son Jesus Christ,
with the Holy Spirit in your holy church,
all honor and glory is yours, almighty God,
    now and for ever.

Amen.

THE LORD'S PRAYER

And now with the confidence of children of God, let us pray: **Our Father…**

BREAKING THE BREAD

The pastor breaks the bread in silence, or while saying:
Because there is one loaf,
we, who are many, are one body, for we all partake of the one loaf.
The bread which we break is a sharing in the body of Christ.

The pastor lifts the cup in silence, or while saying:
The cup over which we give thanks is a sharing in the blood of Christ.

GIVING THE BREAD AND CUP

The bread and cup are given to the people, with these or other words being exchanged:
The body of Christ, given for you. **Amen.**
The blood of Christ, given for you. **Amen.**

PRAYER AFTER RECEIVING

Eternal God, we give you thanks for this holy mystery
    in which you have given yourself to us.
Give us grace to lead us through this new year
    and into your holy kingdom.
Grant that we may go into the world
    in the strength of your Spirit,
    to give ourselves for others.
in the name of Jesus Christ our Lord.
Amen.

Epiphany of the Lord

Isaiah 60:1-6 ; Psalm 72:1-7, 10-14; Ephesians 3:1-12 ; Matthew 2:1-12

The Lord be with you.
And also with you.
Lift up your hearts.
We lift them up to the Lord.
Let us give thanks to the Lord our God.
It is right to give our thanks and praise.

It is right, and a good and joyful thing
    always and everywhere to give thanks to you,
    Almighty God, Creator of heaven and earth.
Your light has come and shines upon us.
Your glory appears over us, calling all the world to you.

And so, with your people on earth
    and all the company of heaven,
    we praise your name and join their unending hymn:

Holy, holy, holy Lord, God of power and might,
heaven and earth are full of your glory.
    Hosanna in the highest.
Blessed is he who comes in the name of the Lord.
    Hosanna in the highest.

Holy are you, and blessed is your Son Jesus Christ.
He defends the cause of the poor,
    gives deliverance to the needy, and crushes the oppressor.
He has pity on the weak, and saves the lives of those in need.
He redeems their lives from oppression and violence.
Precious is their blood in his sight.

Your Spirit anointed him
    to preach good news to the poor,
    to proclaim release to the captives and
    recovering of sight to the blind,
    to set at liberty those who are oppressed, and
    to announce that the time had come
    when you would save your people.
He healed the sick, fed the hungry, and ate with sinners.

By the baptism of his suffering, death, and resurrection,
    you gave birth to your church,
    delivered us from slavery to sin and death,
    and made with us a new covenant
    by water and the Spirit.

On the night in which he gave himself up for us
    he took bread, gave thanks to you, broke the bread,
    gave it to his disciples, and said,
"Take, eat; this is my body which is given for you.
Do this in remembrance of me."

When the supper was over he took the cup,
    gave thanks to you, gave it to his disciples, and said,
"Drink from this, all of you; this is my blood of the
    new covenant poured out for you and for many
        for the forgiveness of sins.
Do this as often as you drink it,
    in remembrance of me."

And so, in remembrance of these your mighty acts in Jesus Christ,
we offer ourselves in praise and thanksgiving
    as a holy and living sacrifice,
    in union with Christ's offering for us,
as we proclaim the mystery of faith.

Christ has died; Christ is risen; Christ will come again.

Pour out your Holy Spirit on us gathered here,
    and on these gifts of bread and wine.
Make them be for us the body and blood of Christ,
that we may be for the world the body of Christ,
    redeemed by his blood,
that all might be illuminated by the light of Christ.

By your Spirit make us one with Christ,
    one with each other and
    one in ministry to all the world,
until Christ comes in final victory and
    we feast at the heavenly banquet.

Through your Son Jesus Christ,
with the Holy Spirit in your holy church,
all honor and glory is yours, almighty God,
    now and for ever.

Amen.

THE LORD'S PRAYER

And now with the confidence of children of God, let us pray: **Our Father...**

BREAKING THE BREAD

The pastor breaks the bread in silence, or while saying:
Because there is one loaf,
we, who are many, are one body, for we all partake of the one loaf.
The bread which we break is a sharing in the body of Christ.

The pastor lifts the cup in silence, or while saying:
The cup over which we give thanks is a sharing in the blood of Christ.

GIVING THE BREAD AND CUP

The bread and cup are given to the people, with these or other words being exchanged:
The body of Christ, given for you. **Amen.**
The blood of Christ, given for you. **Amen.**

PRAYER AFTER RECEIVING

Eternal God, we give you thanks for this holy mystery
    in which you have given yourself to us.
Through this sacrament we know you
    and have access to you in boldness and confidence.
Grant that we may go into the world
    in the strength of your Spirit,
    to give ourselves for others.
in the name of Jesus Christ our Lord.
Amen.

Baptism of the Lord (a)

Isaiah 42:1-9; Psalm 29; Acts 10:34-43; Matthew 3:13-17

The Lord be with you.
And also with you.
Lift up your hearts.
We lift them up to the Lord.
Let us give thanks to the Lord our God.
It is right to give our thanks and praise.

It is right, and a good and joyful thing
    always and everywhere to give thanks to you,
    Almighty God, Creator of heaven and earth.
You have given us your servant
    whom you have called in righteousness.
Through him the former things have come to pass,
    and new things spring forth at your word.

And so, with your people on earth
    and all the company of heaven,
    we praise your name and join their unending hymn:

Holy, holy, holy Lord, God of power and might,
heaven and earth are full of your glory.
    Hosanna in the highest.
Blessed is he who comes in the name of the Lord.
    Hosanna in the highest.

Holy are you, and blessed is your Son Jesus Christ.
At his baptism your Spirit came upon him
    to bring all the nations to you.

Your Spirit anointed him
    to preach good news to the poor,
    to proclaim release to the captives and
    recovering of sight to the blind,
    to set at liberty those who are oppressed, and
    to announce that the time had come
    when you would save your people.
He healed the sick, fed the hungry, and ate with sinners.

By the baptism of his suffering, death, and resurrection,
  you gave birth to your church,
  delivered us from slavery to sin and death,
  and made with us a new covenant
  by water and the Spirit.

On the night in which he gave himself up for us
  he took bread, gave thanks to you, broke the bread,
  gave it to his disciples, and said,
"Take, eat; this is my body which is given for you.
Do this in remembrance of me."

When the supper was over he took the cup,
  gave thanks to you, gave it to his disciples, and said,
"Drink from this, all of you; this is my blood of the
    new covenant poured out for you and for many
      for the forgiveness of sins.
Do this as often as you drink it,
  in remembrance of me."

And so, in remembrance of these your mighty acts in Jesus Christ,
we offer ourselves in praise and thanksgiving
  as a holy and living sacrifice,
  in union with Christ's offering for us,
as we proclaim the mystery of faith.

Christ has died; Christ is risen; Christ will come again.

Pour out your Holy Spirit on us gathered here,
  and on these gifts of bread and wine.
Make them be for us the body and blood of Christ,
that we may be for the world the body of Christ,
  redeemed by his blood,
      that we might be witnesses to him.

By your Spirit make us one with Christ,
  one with each other and
  one in ministry to all the world,
until Christ comes in final victory and
  we feast at the heavenly banquet.

Through your Son Jesus Christ,
with the Holy Spirit in your holy church,
all honor and glory is yours, almighty God,
    now and for ever.

Amen.

THE LORD'S PRAYER
And now with the confidence of children of God, let us pray: **Our Father...**

BREAKING THE BREAD
The pastor breaks the bread in silence, or while saying:
Because there is one loaf,
we, who are many, are one body, for we all partake of the one loaf.
The bread which we break is a sharing in the body of Christ.

The pastor lifts the cup in silence, or while saying:
The cup over which we give thanks is a sharing in the blood of Christ.

GIVING THE BREAD AND CUP
The bread and cup are given to the people, with these or other words being exchanged:
The body of Christ, given for you. **Amen.**
The blood of Christ, given for you. **Amen.**

PRAYER AFTER RECEIVING
Eternal God, we give you thanks for this holy mystery
    in which you have given yourself to us.
On this day remind us again of our baptism and
    the grace that comes through it.
Grant that we may go into the world
    in the strength of your Spirit,
    to give ourselves for others.
in the name of Jesus Christ our Lord.
Amen.

Second Sunday After the Epiphany (a)

Isaiah 49:1-7; Psalm 40:1-11; 1 Corinthians 1:1-9; John 1:29-42

The Lord be with you.
And also with you.
Lift up your hearts.
We lift them up to the Lord.
Let us give thanks to the Lord our God.
It is right to give our thanks and praise.

It is right, and a good and joyful thing
    always and everywhere to give thanks to you,
    Almighty God, Creator of heaven and earth.
You are the Redeemed, the Holy One
    whom we worship and adore.
Even kings and leaders of nations are humbled before you.

And so, with your people on earth
    and all the company of heaven,
    we praise your name and join their unending hymn:

Holy, holy, holy Lord, God of power and might,
heaven and earth are full of your glory.
    Hosanna in the highest.
Blessed is he who comes in the name of the Lord.
    Hosanna in the highest.

Holy are you, and blessed is your Son Jesus Christ.
You have empowered him with your Spirit
    to be your Lamb
        who takes away the sins of the world.

Your Spirit anointed him
    to preach good news to the poor,
    to proclaim release to the captives and
    recovering of sight to the blind,
    to set at liberty those who are oppressed, and
    to announce that the time had come
    when you would save your people.
He healed the sick, fed the hungry, and ate with sinners.

By the baptism of his suffering, death, and resurrection,
    you gave birth to your church,
    delivered us from slavery to sin and death,
    and made with us a new covenant
    by water and the Spirit.

On the night in which he gave himself up for us
    he took bread, gave thanks to you, broke the bread,
    gave it to his disciples, and said,
"Take, eat; this is my body which is given for you.
Do this in remembrance of me."

When the supper was over he took the cup,
    gave thanks to you, gave it to his disciples, and said,
"Drink from this, all of you; this is my blood of the
    new covenant poured out for you and for many
        for the forgiveness of sins.
Do this as often as you drink it,
    in remembrance of me."

And so, in remembrance of these your mighty acts in Jesus Christ,
we offer ourselves in praise and thanksgiving
    as a holy and living sacrifice,
    in union with Christ's offering for us,
as we proclaim the mystery of faith.

Christ has died; Christ is risen; Christ will come again.

Pour out your Holy Spirit on us gathered here,
    and on these gifts of bread and wine.
Make them be for us the body and blood of Christ,
that we may be for the world the body of Christ,
    redeemed by his blood,
        that it may strengthen us to the end.

By your Spirit make us one with Christ,
    one with each other and
    one in ministry to all the world,
until Christ comes in final victory and
    we feast at the heavenly banquet.

Through your Son Jesus Christ,
with the Holy Spirit in your holy church,
all honor and glory is yours, almighty God,
     now and for ever.

Amen.

THE LORD'S PRAYER

And now with the confidence of children of God, let us pray: **Our Father...**

BREAKING THE BREAD

The pastor breaks the bread in silence, or while saying:
Because there is one loaf,
we, who are many, are one body, for we all partake of the one loaf.
The bread which we break is a sharing in the body of Christ.

The pastor lifts the cup in silence, or while saying:
The cup over which we give thanks is a sharing in the blood of Christ.

GIVING THE BREAD AND CUP

The bread and cup are given to the people, with these or other words being exchanged:
The body of Christ, given for you. **Amen.**
The blood of Christ, given for you. **Amen.**

PRAYER AFTER RECEIVING

Eternal God, we give you thanks for this holy mystery
     in which you have given yourself to us,
          and for the grace given us.
Grant that we may go into the world
     in the strength of your Spirit,
          to give ourselves for others.
in the name of Jesus Christ our Lord.
Amen.

Third Sunday After the Epiphany (a)

Isaiah 9:1-4; Psalm 27:1, 4-9; 1 Corinthians 1:10-18; Matthew 4:12-23

The Lord be with you.
And also with you.
Lift up your hearts.
We lift them up to the Lord.
Let us give thanks to the Lord our God.
It is right to give our thanks and praise.

It is right, and a good and joyful thing
    always and everywhere to give thanks to you,
      Almighty God, Creator of heaven and earth.
Your promises are wonderful, O Lord.
The people who walked in darkness have seen a great light;
    those who lived in a land of deep darkness
      --on them has light shined.
You have multiplied the nation and increased its joy.

And so, with your people on earth
    and all the company of heaven,
    we praise your name and join their unending hymn:

Holy, holy, holy Lord, God of power and might,
heaven and earth are full of your glory.
    Hosanna in the highest.
Blessed is he who comes in the name of the Lord.
    Hosanna in the highest.

Holy are you, and blessed is your Son Jesus Christ.
He is the light of the world
    and delivers us from darkness.

Your Spirit anointed him
    to preach good news to the poor,
    to proclaim release to the captives and
    recovering of sight to the blind,
    to set at liberty those who are oppressed, and
    to announce that the time had come
    when you would save your people.
He healed the sick, fed the hungry, and ate with sinners.

By the baptism of his suffering, death, and resurrection,
    you gave birth to your church,
    delivered us from slavery to sin and death,
    and made with us a new covenant
    by water and the Spirit.

On the night in which he gave himself up for us
    he took bread, gave thanks to you, broke the bread,
    gave it to his disciples, and said,
"Take, eat; this is my body which is given for you.
Do this in remembrance of me."

When the supper was over he took the cup,
    gave thanks to you, gave it to his disciples, and said,
"Drink from this, all of you; this is my blood of the
    new covenant poured out for you and for many
        for the forgiveness of sins.
Do this as often as you drink it,
    in remembrance of me."

And so, in remembrance of these your mighty acts in Jesus Christ,
we offer ourselves in praise and thanksgiving
    as a holy and living sacrifice,
    in union with Christ's offering for us,
as we proclaim the mystery of faith.

Christ has died; Christ is risen; Christ will come again.

Pour out your Holy Spirit on us gathered here,
    and on these gifts of bread and wine.
Make them be for us the body and blood of Christ,
that we may be for the world the body of Christ,
    redeemed by his blood,
that we might understand the foolishness of the cross
    and be saved by your power.

By your Spirit make us one with Christ,
    one with each other and
    one in ministry to all the world,
until Christ comes in final victory and
    we feast at the heavenly banquet.

Through your Son Jesus Christ,
with the Holy Spirit in your holy church,
all honor and glory is yours, almighty God,
     now and for ever.

Amen.

THE LORD'S PRAYER

And now with the confidence of children of God, let us pray: **Our Father...**

BREAKING THE BREAD

The pastor breaks the bread in silence, or while saying:
Because there is one loaf,
we, who are many, are one body, for we all partake of the one loaf.
The bread which we break is a sharing in the body of Christ.

The pastor lifts the cup in silence, or while saying:
The cup over which we give thanks is a sharing in the blood of Christ.

GIVING THE BREAD AND CUP

The bread and cup are given to the people, with these or other words being exchanged:
The body of Christ, given for you. **Amen.**
The blood of Christ, given for you. **Amen.**

PRAYER AFTER RECEIVING

Eternal God, we give you thanks for this holy mystery
     in which you have given yourself to us.
We pray that we might follow Jesus faithfully all our days.
Grant that we may go into the world
     in the strength of your Spirit,
     to give ourselves for others.
in the name of Jesus Christ our Lord.
Amen.

Fourth Sunday After the Epiphany (a)

Micah 6:1-8; Psalm 15; 1 Corinthians 1:18-31; Matthew 5:1-12

The Lord be with you.
And also with you.
Lift up your hearts.
We lift them up to the Lord.
Let us give thanks to the Lord our God.
It is right to give our thanks and praise.

It is right, and a good and joyful thing
    always and everywhere to give thanks to you,
    Almighty God, Creator of heaven and earth.
Your foolishness
    is greater than human wisdom
and your weakness
    is stronger than human strength.

And so, with your people on earth
    and all the company of heaven,
    we praise your name and join their unending hymn:

Holy, holy, holy Lord, God of power and might,
heaven and earth are full of your glory.
    Hosanna in the highest.
Blessed is he who comes in the name of the Lord.
    Hosanna in the highest.

Holy are you, and blessed is your Son Jesus Christ.
He is your wisdom made flesh;
    your righteousness
        and sanctification and redemption.

Your Spirit anointed him
    to preach good news to the poor,
    to proclaim release to the captives and
    recovering of sight to the blind,
    to set at liberty those who are oppressed, and
    to announce that the time had come
    when you would save your people.
He healed the sick, fed the hungry, and ate with sinners.

By the baptism of his suffering, death, and resurrection,
    you gave birth to your church,
    delivered us from slavery to sin and death,
    and made with us a new covenant
    by water and the Spirit.

On the night in which he gave himself up for us
    he took bread, gave thanks to you, broke the bread,
    gave it to his disciples, and said,
"Take, eat; this is my body which is given for you.
Do this in remembrance of me."

When the supper was over he took the cup,
    gave thanks to you, gave it to his disciples, and said,
"Drink from this, all of you; this is my blood of the
    new covenant poured out for you and for many
        for the forgiveness of sins.
Do this as often as you drink it,
    in remembrance of me."

And so, in remembrance of these your mighty acts in Jesus Christ,
we offer ourselves in praise and thanksgiving
    as a holy and living sacrifice,
    in union with Christ's offering for us,
as we proclaim the mystery of faith.

Christ has died; Christ is risen; Christ will come again.

Pour out your Holy Spirit on us gathered here,
    and on these gifts of bread and wine.
Make them be for us the body and blood of Christ,
that we may be for the world the body of Christ,
    redeemed by his blood.
that we might do justice and love kindness
    and walk humbly with you, our God.

By your Spirit make us one with Christ,
    one with each other and
    one in ministry to all the world,
until Christ comes in final victory and
    we feast at the heavenly banquet.

Through your Son Jesus Christ,
with the Holy Spirit in your holy church,
all honor and glory is yours, almighty God,
    now and for ever.

Amen.

THE LORD'S PRAYER

And now with the confidence of children of God, let us pray: **Our Father...**

BREAKING THE BREAD

The pastor breaks the bread in silence, or while saying:
Because there is one loaf,
we, who are many, are one body, for we all partake of the one loaf.
The bread which we break is a sharing in the body of Christ.

The pastor lifts the cup in silence, or while saying:
The cup over which we give thanks is a sharing in the blood of Christ.

GIVING THE BREAD AND CUP

The bread and cup are given to the people, with these or other words being exchanged:
The body of Christ, given for you. **Amen.**
The blood of Christ, given for you. **Amen.**

PRAYER AFTER RECEIVING

Eternal God, we give you thanks for this holy mystery
    in which you have given yourself to us.
Make us ever faithful to your high calling of love and justice.
Grant that we may go into the world
    in the strength of your Spirit,
        to give ourselves for others.
in the name of Jesus Christ our Lord.
Amen.

*NOTE: Benediction from Micah 6:8 (see page 223) is especially appropriate this
        Sunday.*

Fifth Sunday After the Epiphany (a)

Isaiah 58:1-9a, (9b-12); Psalm 112:1-9, (10); 1 Corinthians 2:1-12, (13-16); Matthew 5:13-20

The Lord be with you.
And also with you.
Lift up your hearts.
We lift them up to the Lord.
Let us give thanks to the Lord our God.
It is right to give our thanks and praise.

It is right, and a good and joyful thing
    always and everywhere to give thanks to you,
    Almighty God, Creator of heaven and earth.
You guide us and satisfy our needs.
You make our bones strong.
You call upon us to offer meaningful sacrifices
    that feed the poor, house the homeless,
        and clothe the naked.

And so, with your people on earth
    and all the company of heaven,
    we praise your name and join their unending hymn:

Holy, holy, holy Lord, God of power and might,
heaven and earth are full of your glory.
    Hosanna in the highest.
Blessed is he who comes in the name of the Lord.
    Hosanna in the highest.

Holy are you, and blessed is your Son Jesus Christ.
He is your wisdom revealed to the world,
    decreed before the ages to those who had ears to hear.

Your Spirit anointed him
    to preach good news to the poor,
    to proclaim release to the captives and
    recovering of sight to the blind,
    to set at liberty those who are oppressed, and
    to announce that the time had come
    when you would save your people.
He healed the sick, fed the hungry, and ate with sinners.

By the baptism of his suffering, death, and resurrection,
    you gave birth to your church,
    delivered us from slavery to sin and death,
    and made with us a new covenant
    by water and the Spirit.

On the night in which he gave himself up for us
    he took bread, gave thanks to you, broke the bread,
    gave it to his disciples, and said,
"Take, eat; this is my body which is given for you.
Do this in remembrance of me."

When the supper was over he took the cup,
    gave thanks to you, gave it to his disciples, and said,
"Drink from this, all of you; this is my blood of the
    new covenant poured out for you and for many
        for the forgiveness of sins.
Do this as often as you drink it,
    in remembrance of me."

And so, in remembrance of these your mighty acts in Jesus Christ,
we offer ourselves in praise and thanksgiving
    as a holy and living sacrifice,
    in union with Christ's offering for us,
as we proclaim the mystery of faith.

Christ has died; Christ is risen; Christ will come again.

Pour out your Holy Spirit on us gathered here,
    and on these gifts of bread and wine.
Make them be for us the body and blood of Christ,
that we may be for the world the body of Christ,
    redeemed by his blood,
that we might know your wisdom
    and apply it to all in need.

By your Spirit make us one with Christ,
    one with each other and
    one in ministry to all the world,
until Christ comes in final victory and
    we feast at the heavenly banquet.

Through your Son Jesus Christ,
with the Holy Spirit in your holy church,
all honor and glory is yours, almighty God,
    now and for ever.

Amen.

THE LORD'S PRAYER

And now with the confidence of children of God, let us pray: **Our Father...**

BREAKING THE BREAD

The pastor breaks the bread in silence, or while saying:
Because there is one loaf,
we, who are many, are one body, for we all partake of the one loaf.
The bread which we break is a sharing in the body of Christ.

The pastor lifts the cup in silence, or while saying:
The cup over which we give thanks is a sharing in the blood of Christ.

GIVING THE BREAD AND CUP

The bread and cup are given to the people, with these or other words being exchanged:
The body of Christ, given for you. **Amen.**
The blood of Christ, given for you. **Amen.**

PRAYER AFTER RECEIVING

Eternal God, we give you thanks for this holy mystery
    in which you have given yourself to us.
You have called us
    through this sacrifice
        to be a sacrifice.
Grant that we may go into the world
    in the strength of your Spirit,
        to give ourselves for others.
in the name of Jesus Christ our Lord.
Amen.

Deuteronomy 30:15-20; Psalm 119:1-8; 1 Corinthians 3:1-9; Matthew 5:21-37

The Lord be with you.
And also with you.
Lift up your hearts.
We lift them up to the Lord.
Let us give thanks to the Lord our God.
It is right to give our thanks and praise.

It is right, and a good and joyful thing
    always and everywhere to give thanks to you,
      Almighty God, Creator of heaven and earth.
You have shown us that
    by living by your Law
we have been given the way
    of life and prosperity.

And so, with your people on earth
    and all the company of heaven,
    we praise your name and join their unending hymn:

Holy, holy, holy Lord, God of power and might,
heaven and earth are full of your glory.
    Hosanna in the highest.
Blessed is he who comes in the name of the Lord.
    Hosanna in the highest.

Holy are you, and blessed is your Son Jesus Christ.
He has shown us the way to life
    through reconciliation and love.

Your Spirit anointed him
    to preach good news to the poor,
    to proclaim release to the captives and
    recovering of sight to the blind,
    to set at liberty those who are oppressed, and
    to announce that the time had come
    when you would save your people.
He healed the sick, fed the hungry, and ate with sinners.

By the baptism of his suffering, death, and resurrection,
    you gave birth to your church,
    delivered us from slavery to sin and death,
    and made with us a new covenant
    by water and the Spirit.

On the night in which he gave himself up for us
    he took bread, gave thanks to you, broke the bread,
    gave it to his disciples, and said,
"Take, eat; this is my body which is given for you.
Do this in remembrance of me."

When the supper was over he took the cup,
    gave thanks to you, gave it to his disciples, and said,
"Drink from this, all of you; this is my blood of the
    new covenant poured out for you and for many
        for the forgiveness of sins.
Do this as often as you drink it,
    in remembrance of me."

And so, in remembrance of these your mighty acts in Jesus Christ,
we offer ourselves in praise and thanksgiving
    as a holy and living sacrifice,
    in union with Christ's offering for us,
as we proclaim the mystery of faith.

Christ has died; Christ is risen; Christ will come again.

Pour out your Holy Spirit on us gathered here,
    and on these gifts of bread and wine.
Make them be for us the body and blood of Christ,
that we may be for the world the body of Christ,
    redeemed by his blood,
that we might be agents
    of reconciliation and love.

By your Spirit make us one with Christ,
    one with each other and
    one in ministry to all the world,
until Christ comes in final victory and
    we feast at the heavenly banquet.

Through your Son Jesus Christ,
with the Holy Spirit in your holy church,
all honor and glory is yours, almighty God,
    now and for ever.

Amen.

THE LORD'S PRAYER

And now with the confidence of children of God, let us pray: **Our Father…**

BREAKING THE BREAD

The pastor breaks the bread in silence, or while saying:
Because there is one loaf,
we, who are many, are one body, for we all partake of the one loaf.
The bread which we break is a sharing in the body of Christ.

The pastor lifts the cup in silence, or while saying:
The cup over which we give thanks is a sharing in the blood of Christ.

GIVING THE BREAD AND CUP

The bread and cup are given to the people, with these or other words being exchanged:
The body of Christ, given for you. **Amen.**
The blood of Christ, given for you. **Amen.**

PRAYER AFTER RECEIVING

Eternal God, we give you thanks for this holy mystery
    in which you have given yourself to us.
Help us live as those freed by your Law
    and not confined by it.
Grant that we may go into the world
    in the strength of your Spirit,
        to give ourselves for others.
in the name of Jesus Christ our Lord.
Amen.

Seventh Sunday After the Epiphany (a)

Leviticus 19:1-2, 9-18; Psalm 119:33-40; 1 Corinthians 3:10-11, 16-23; Matthew 5:38-48

The Lord be with you.
And also with you.
Lift up your hearts.
We lift them up to the Lord.
Let us give thanks to the Lord our God.
It is right to give our thanks and praise.

It is right, and a good and joyful thing
    always and everywhere to give thanks to you,
      Almighty God, Creator of heaven and earth.
You taught your people to honor one another,
    to provide for the needy
        and to be honest in all things.

And so, with your people on earth
    and all the company of heaven,
    we praise your name and join their unending hymn:

Holy, holy, holy Lord, God of power and might,
heaven and earth are full of your glory.
    Hosanna in the highest.
Blessed is he who comes in the name of the Lord.
    Hosanna in the highest.

Holy are you, and blessed is your Son Jesus Christ.
He moves us beyond the letter of the Law
    to the spirit of the law
        and deepens its meaning.

Your Spirit anointed him
    to preach good news to the poor,
    to proclaim release to the captives and
    recovering of sight to the blind,
    to set at liberty those who are oppressed, and
    to announce that the time had come
    when you would save your people.
He healed the sick, fed the hungry, and ate with sinners.

By the baptism of his suffering, death, and resurrection,
    you gave birth to your church,
    delivered us from slavery to sin and death,
    and made with us a new covenant
    by water and the Spirit.

On the night in which he gave himself up for us
    he took bread, gave thanks to you, broke the bread,
    gave it to his disciples, and said,
"Take, eat; this is my body which is given for you.
Do this in remembrance of me."

When the supper was over he took the cup,
    gave thanks to you, gave it to his disciples, and said,
"Drink from this, all of you; this is my blood of the
    new covenant poured out for you and for many
        for the forgiveness of sins.
Do this as often as you drink it,
    in remembrance of me."

And so, in remembrance of these your mighty acts in Jesus Christ,
we offer ourselves in praise and thanksgiving
    as a holy and living sacrifice,
    in union with Christ's offering for us,
as we proclaim the mystery of faith.

Christ has died; Christ is risen; Christ will come again.

Pour out your Holy Spirit on us gathered here,
    and on these gifts of bread and wine.
Make them be for us the body and blood of Christ,
that we may be for the world the body of Christ,
    redeemed by his blood,
for we are your temple
    and your spirit dwells within us.

By your Spirit make us one with Christ,
    one with each other and
    one in ministry to all the world,
until Christ comes in final victory and
    we feast at the heavenly banquet.

56

O'Donnell, *Lift Up Your Hearts 3rd ed. Year A*

Through your Son Jesus Christ,
with the Holy Spirit in your holy church,
all honor and glory is yours, almighty God,
     now and for ever.

Amen.

THE LORD'S PRAYER
And now with the confidence of children of God, let us pray: **Our Father...**

BREAKING THE BREAD
The pastor breaks the bread in silence, or while saying:
Because there is one loaf,
we, who are many, are one body, for we all partake of the one loaf.
The bread which we break is a sharing in the body of Christ.

The pastor lifts the cup in silence, or while saying:
The cup over which we give thanks is a sharing in the blood of Christ.

GIVING THE BREAD AND CUP
The bread and cup are given to the people, with these or other words being exchanged:
The body of Christ, given for you. **Amen.**
The blood of Christ, given for you. **Amen.**

PRAYER AFTER RECEIVING
Eternal God, we give you thanks for this holy mystery
     in which you have given yourself to us.
Make us agents of love, peace, harmony, and justice.
Grant that we may go into the world
     in the strength of your Spirit,
     to give ourselves for others.
in the name of Jesus Christ our Lord.
Amen.

Eighth Sunday After the Epiphany (a)

Isaiah 49:8-16a; Psalm 131; 1 Corinthians 4:1-5; Matthew 6:24-34

The Lord be with you.
And also with you.
Lift up your hearts.
We lift them up to the Lord.
Let us give thanks to the Lord our God.
It is right to give our thanks and praise.

It is right, and a good and joyful thing
    always and everywhere to give thanks to you,
    Almighty God, Creator of heaven and earth.
Even in the darkest of days, you do not forget us
    as a mother never forgets her nursing child.
You comfort your people
    and have compassion on all who suffer.

And so, with your people on earth
    and all the company of heaven,
    we praise your name and join their unending hymn:

Holy, holy, holy Lord, God of power and might,
heaven and earth are full of your glory.
    Hosanna in the highest.
Blessed is he who comes in the name of the Lord.
    Hosanna in the highest.

Holy are you, and blessed is your Son Jesus Christ.
He has shown us the deeper meaning of life
    and that we cannot server two masters.

Your Spirit anointed him
    to preach good news to the poor,
    to proclaim release to the captives and
    recovering of sight to the blind,
    to set at liberty those who are oppressed, and
    to announce that the time had come
    when you would save your people.
He healed the sick, fed the hungry, and ate with sinners.

By the baptism of his suffering, death, and resurrection,
    you gave birth to your church,
    delivered us from slavery to sin and death,
    and made with us a new covenant
    by water and the Spirit.

On the night in which he gave himself up for us
    he took bread, gave thanks to you, broke the bread,
    gave it to his disciples, and said,
"Take, eat; this is my body which is given for you.
Do this in remembrance of me."

When the supper was over he took the cup,
    gave thanks to you, gave it to his disciples, and said,
"Drink from this, all of you; this is my blood of the
    new covenant poured out for you and for many
        for the forgiveness of sins.
Do this as often as you drink it,
    in remembrance of me."

And so, in remembrance of these your mighty acts in Jesus Christ,
we offer ourselves in praise and thanksgiving
    as a holy and living sacrifice,
    in union with Christ's offering for us,
as we proclaim the mystery of faith.

Christ has died; Christ is risen; Christ will come again.

Pour out your Holy Spirit on us gathered here,
    and on these gifts of bread and wine.
Make them be for us the body and blood of Christ,
that we may be for the world the body of Christ,
    redeemed by his blood,
for we are his servants
    and the stewards of your mysteries.

By your Spirit make us one with Christ,
    one with each other and
    one in ministry to all the world,
until Christ comes in final victory and
    we feast at the heavenly banquet.

Through your Son Jesus Christ,
with the Holy Spirit in your holy church,
all honor and glory is yours, almighty God,
    now and for ever.

Amen.

THE LORD'S PRAYER

And now with the confidence of children of God, let us pray: **Our Father...**

BREAKING THE BREAD

The pastor breaks the bread in silence, or while saying:
Because there is one loaf,
we, who are many, are one body, for we all partake of the one loaf.
The bread which we break is a sharing in the body of Christ.

The pastor lifts the cup in silence, or while saying:
The cup over which we give thanks is a sharing in the blood of Christ.

GIVING THE BREAD AND CUP

The bread and cup are given to the people, with these or other words being exchanged:
The body of Christ, given for you. **Amen.**
The blood of Christ, given for you. **Amen.**

PRAYER AFTER RECEIVING

Eternal God, we give you thanks for this holy mystery
    in which you have given yourself to us.
Help us set aside our worldly concerns
    and do what is righteous in your sight.
Grant that we may go into the world
    in the strength of your Spirit,
       to give ourselves for others.
in the name of Jesus Christ our Lord.
Amen.

Transfiguration Sunday (a)

Exodus 24:12-18; Psalm 2 (or 99); 2 Peter1:16-21; Matthew 17:1-9

The Lord be with you.
And also with you.
Lift up your hearts.
We lift them up to the Lord.
Let us give thanks to the Lord our God.
It is right to give our thanks and praise.

It is right, and a good and joyful thing
    always and everywhere to give thanks to you,
    Almighty God, Creator of heaven and earth.
Through Moses you revealed yourself
    and gave us the Law.
Through Elijah you told
    of your desire for us.

And so, with your people on earth
    and all the company of heaven,
    we praise your name and join their unending hymn:

Holy, holy, holy Lord, God of power and might,
heaven and earth are full of your glory.
    Hosanna in the highest.
Blessed is he who comes in the name of the Lord.
    Hosanna in the highest.

Holy are you, and blessed is your Son Jesus Christ.
You revealed his holy nature
    when he was transfigured
        before Peter and James and John.

Your Spirit anointed him
    to preach good news to the poor,
    to proclaim release to the captives and
    recovering of sight to the blind,
    to set at liberty those who are oppressed, and
    to announce that the time had come
    when you would save your people.
He healed the sick, fed the hungry, and ate with sinners.

By the baptism of his suffering, death, and resurrection,
    you gave birth to your church,
    delivered us from slavery to sin and death,
    and made with us a new covenant
    by water and the Spirit.

On the night in which he gave himself up for us
    he took bread, gave thanks to you, broke the bread,
    gave it to his disciples, and said,
"Take, eat; this is my body which is given for you.
Do this in remembrance of me."

When the supper was over he took the cup,
    gave thanks to you, gave it to his disciples, and said,
"Drink from this, all of you; this is my blood of the
    new covenant poured out for you and for many
        for the forgiveness of sins.
Do this as often as you drink it,
    in remembrance of me."

And so, in remembrance of these your mighty acts in Jesus Christ,
we offer ourselves in praise and thanksgiving
    as a holy and living sacrifice,
    in union with Christ's offering for us,
as we proclaim the mystery of faith.

Christ has died; Christ is risen; Christ will come again.

Pour out your Holy Spirit on us gathered here,
    and on these gifts of bread and wine.
Make them be for us the body and blood of Christ,
that we may be for the world the body of Christ,
    redeemed by his blood,
for he the Law and the prophets complete.

By your Spirit make us one with Christ,
    one with each other and
    one in ministry to all the world,
until Christ comes in final victory and
    we feast at the heavenly banquet.

Through your Son Jesus Christ,
with the Holy Spirit in your holy church,
all honor and glory is yours, almighty God,
    now and for ever.

Amen.

THE LORD'S PRAYER

And now with the confidence of children of God, let us pray: **Our Father...**

BREAKING THE BREAD

The pastor breaks the bread in silence, or while saying:
Because there is one loaf,
we, who are many, are one body, for we all partake of the one loaf.
The bread which we break is a sharing in the body of Christ.

The pastor lifts the cup in silence, or while saying:
The cup over which we give thanks is a sharing in the blood of Christ.

GIVING THE BREAD AND CUP

The bread and cup are given to the people, with these or other words being exchanged:
The body of Christ, given for you. **Amen.**
The blood of Christ, given for you. **Amen.**

PRAYER AFTER RECEIVING

Eternal God, we give you thanks for this holy mystery
    in which you have given yourself to us.
Help us discover that which is holy within us.
Grant that we may go into the world
    in the strength of your Spirit,
    to give ourselves for others.
in the name of Jesus Christ our Lord.
Amen.

John and Charles Wesley [March 2]

Isaiah 49:1-6; Romans 12:9-20; Luke 9:2-6

The Lord be with you.
And also with you.
Lift up your hearts.
We lift them up to the Lord.
Let us give thanks to the Lord our God.
It is right to give our thanks and praise.

It is right, and a good and joyful thing
    always and everywhere to give thanks to you,
      Almighty God, Creator of heaven and earth.
You called forth your servant from the womb
    to bring your people back to you
    and to bring the message of salvation to all the world.

And so, with your people on earth
    and all the company of heaven,
    we praise your name and join their unending hymn:

Holy, holy, holy Lord, God of power and might,
heaven and earth are full of your glory.
    Hosanna in the highest.
Blessed is he who comes in the name of the Lord.
    Hosanna in the highest.

Holy are you, and blessed is your Son Jesus Christ.
He is the light of the nations.
He sent out his disciples to heal
    and proclaim your love to all the world.

Your Spirit anointed him
    to preach good news to the poor,
    to proclaim release to the captives and
    recovering of sight to the blind,
    to set at liberty those who are oppressed, and
    to announce that the time had come
    when you would save your people.
He healed the sick, fed the hungry, and ate with sinners.

By the baptism of his suffering, death, and resurrection,
    you gave birth to your church,
    delivered us from slavery to sin and death,
    and made with us a new covenant
    by water and the Spirit.

On the night in which he gave himself up for us
    he took bread, gave thanks to you, broke the bread,
    gave it to his disciples, and said,
"Take, eat; this is my body which is given for you.
Do this in remembrance of me."

When the supper was over he took the cup,
    gave thanks to you, gave it to his disciples, and said,
"Drink from this, all of you; this is my blood of the
    new covenant poured out for you and for many
        for the forgiveness of sins.
Do this as often as you drink it,
    in remembrance of me."

And so, in remembrance of these your mighty acts in Jesus Christ,
we offer ourselves in praise and thanksgiving
    as a holy and living sacrifice,
    in union with Christ's offering for us,
as we proclaim the mystery of faith.

Christ has died; Christ is risen; Christ will come again.

Pour out your Holy Spirit on us gathered here,
    and on these gifts of bread and wine.
Make them be for us the body and blood of Christ,
that we may be for the world the body of Christ,
    redeemed by his blood,
that we might be empowered by love in all that we do.

By your Spirit make us one with Christ,
    one with each other and
    one in ministry to all the world,
until Christ comes in final victory and
    we feast at the heavenly banquet.

Through your Son Jesus Christ,
with the Holy Spirit in your holy church,
all honor and glory is yours, almighty God,
    now and for ever.

Amen.

THE LORD'S PRAYER
And now with the confidence of children of God, let us pray: **Our Father...**

BREAKING THE BREAD
The pastor breaks the bread in silence, or while saying:
Because there is one loaf,
we, who are many, are one body, for we all partake of the one loaf.
The bread which we break is a sharing in the body of Christ.

The pastor lifts the cup in silence, or while saying:
The cup over which we give thanks is a sharing in the blood of Christ.

GIVING THE BREAD AND CUP
The bread and cup are given to the people, with these or other words being exchanged:
The body of Christ, given for you. **Amen.**
The blood of Christ, given for you. **Amen.**

PRAYER AFTER RECEIVING
Eternal God, we give you thanks for this holy mystery
    in which you have given yourself to us.
Help us to live in harmony with one another,
    that we might live peaceably with all.
Grant that we may go into the world
    in the strength of your Spirit,
    to give ourselves for others.
in the name of Jesus Christ our Lord.
Amen.

Ash Wednesday

Joel 2:1-2, 12-17; Psalm 51:1-17; 2 Corinthians 5:20b-6:10; Matthew 6:1-6, 16-21

The Lord be with you.
And also with you.
Lift up your hearts.
We lift them up to the Lord.
Let us give thanks to the Lord our God.
It is right to give our thanks and praise.

It is right, and a good and joyful thing
    always and everywhere to give thanks to you,
    Almighty God, Creator of heaven and earth.
Even when we rebel and hide from your love
    you are gracious and merciful, abounding in steadfast love;
    for you rejoice in our repentance
       and open to us the gates of your kingdom.

And so, with your people on earth
    and all the company of heaven,
    we praise your name and join their unending hymn:

Holy, holy, holy Lord, God of power and might,
heaven and earth are full of your glory.
    Hosanna in the highest.
Blessed is he who comes in the name of the Lord.
    Hosanna in the highest.

Holy are you, and blessed is your Son Jesus Christ.
He bore our sins that we might be saved,
    and become your righteousness.

Your Spirit anointed him
    to preach good news to the poor,
    to proclaim release to the captives and
    recovering of sight to the blind,
    to set at liberty those who are oppressed, and
    to announce that the time had come
    when you would save your people.
He healed the sick, fed the hungry, and ate with sinners.

By the baptism of his suffering, death, and resurrection,
    you gave birth to your church,
    delivered us from slavery to sin and death,
    and made with us a new covenant
    by water and the Spirit.

On the night in which he gave himself up for us
    he took bread, gave thanks to you, broke the bread,
    gave it to his disciples, and said,
"Take, eat; this is my body which is given for you.
Do this in remembrance of me."

When the supper was over he took the cup,
    gave thanks to you, gave it to his disciples, and said,
"Drink from this, all of you; this is my blood of the
    new covenant poured out for you and for many
        for the forgiveness of sins.
Do this as often as you drink it,
    in remembrance of me."

And so, in remembrance of these your mighty acts in Jesus Christ,
we offer ourselves in praise and thanksgiving
    as a holy and living sacrifice,
    in union with Christ's offering for us,
as we proclaim the mystery of faith.

Christ has died; Christ is risen; Christ will come again.

Pour out your Holy Spirit on us gathered here,
    and on these gifts of bread and wine.
Make them be for us the body and blood of Christ,
that we may be for the world the body of Christ,
    redeemed by his blood
For now is the acceptable time;
    for now is the day of salvation.

By your Spirit make us one with Christ,
    one with each other and
    one in ministry to all the world,
until Christ comes in final victory and
    we feast at the heavenly banquet.

Through your Son Jesus Christ,
with the Holy Spirit in your holy church,
all honor and glory is yours, almighty God,
     now and for ever.

Amen.

THE LORD'S PRAYER

And now with the confidence of children of God, let us pray: **Our Father...**

BREAKING THE BREAD

The pastor breaks the bread in silence, or while saying:
Because there is one loaf,
we, who are many, are one body, for we all partake of the one loaf.
The bread which we break is a sharing in the body of Christ.

The pastor lifts the cup in silence, or while saying:
The cup over which we give thanks is a sharing in the blood of Christ.

GIVING THE BREAD AND CUP

The bread and cup are given to the people, with these or other words being exchanged:
The body of Christ, given for you. **Amen.**
The blood of Christ, given for you. **Amen.**

PRAYER AFTER RECEIVING

Eternal God, we give you thanks for this holy mystery
     in which you have given yourself to us.
Create in us clean hearts
     and put new and right spirits within us.
Grant that we may go into the world
     in the strength of your Spirit,
     to give ourselves for others.
in the name of Jesus Christ our Lord.
Amen.

Genesis 2:15-17, 3:1-7; Psalm32; Romans 5:12-19; Matthew 4:1-11

The Lord be with you.
And also with you.
Lift up your hearts.
We lift them up to the Lord.
Let us give thanks to the Lord our God.
It is right to give our thanks and praise.

It is right, and a good and joyful thing
    always and everywhere to give thanks to you,
      Almighty God, Creator of heaven and earth.
You formed human beings from the dust of the ground
    and breathed life into us.
You gave us a paradise in which to live,
    but we disobeyed you and discovered the difference between good and evil.
Our eyes were opened to behold your true glory.

And so, with your people on earth
    and all the company of heaven,
    we praise your name and join their unending hymn:

Holy, holy, holy Lord, God of power and might,
heaven and earth are full of your glory.
    Hosanna in the highest.
Blessed is he who comes in the name of the Lord.
    Hosanna in the highest.

Holy are you, and blessed is your Son Jesus Christ.
Forty day and forty nights he was tempted in the wilderness.
Yet he renounced all efforts by the tempter to win his obedience.
He died, not for his sins, but for ours.

Your Spirit anointed him
    to preach good news to the poor,
    to proclaim release to the captives and
    recovering of sight to the blind,
    to set at liberty those who are oppressed, and
    to announce that the time had come
    when you would save your people.

He healed the sick, fed the hungry, and ate with sinners.

By the baptism of his suffering, death, and resurrection,
  you gave birth to your church,
  delivered us from slavery to sin and death,
  and made with us a new covenant
  by water and the Spirit.

On the night in which he gave himself up for us
  he took bread, gave thanks to you, broke the bread,
  gave it to his disciples, and said,
"Take, eat; this is my body which is given for you.
Do this in remembrance of me."

When the supper was over he took the cup,
  gave thanks to you, gave it to his disciples, and said,
"Drink from this, all of you; this is my blood of the
  new covenant poured out for you and for many
    for the forgiveness of sins.
Do this as often as you drink it,
  in remembrance of me."

And so, in remembrance of these your mighty acts in Jesus Christ,
we offer ourselves in praise and thanksgiving
  as a holy and living sacrifice,
  in union with Christ's offering for us,
as we proclaim the mystery of faith.

Christ has died; Christ is risen; Christ will come again.

Pour out your Holy Spirit on us gathered here,
  and on these gifts of bread and wine.
Make them be for us the body and blood of Christ,
that we may be for the world the body of Christ,
  redeemed by his blood,
for as by one man
  sin came into the world,
by one man
  sin has been conquered.

By your Spirit make us one with Christ,
    one with each other and
    one in ministry to all the world,
until Christ comes in final victory and
    we feast at the heavenly banquet.

Through your Son Jesus Christ,
with the Holy Spirit in your holy church,
all honor and glory is yours, almighty God,
    now and for ever.

Amen.

THE LORD'S PRAYER

And now with the confidence of children of God, let us pray: **Our Father...**

BREAKING THE BREAD

The pastor breaks the bread in silence, or while saying:
Because there is one loaf,
we, who are many, are one body, for we all partake of the one loaf.
The bread which we break is a sharing in the body of Christ.

The pastor lifts the cup in silence, or while saying:
The cup over which we give thanks is a sharing in the blood of Christ.

GIVING THE BREAD AND CUP

The bread and cup are given to the people, with these or other words being exchanged:
The body of Christ, given for you. **Amen.**
The blood of Christ, given for you. **Amen.**

PRAYER AFTER RECEIVING

Eternal God, we give you thanks for this holy mystery
    in which you have given yourself to us.
Help us use this sacrament and this season of Lent
    to grow closer to you.
Grant that we may go into the world
    in the strength of your Spirit,
        to give ourselves for others.
in the name of Jesus Christ our Lord.
Amen.

Second Sunday in Lent (a)

Genesis 12:1-4a; Psalm 121; Romans 4:1-5, 13-17; John 3:1-17 or Matthew 17:1-9

The Lord be with you.
And also with you.
Lift up your hearts.
We lift them up to the Lord.
Let us give thanks to the Lord our God.
It is right to give our thanks and praise.

It is right, and a good and joyful thing
    always and everywhere to give thanks to you,
    Almighty God, Creator of heaven and earth.
You promised Abram
    that he would father a great nation,
        a holy nation,
and that we would be your heirs in faith.

And so, with your people on earth
    and all the company of heaven,
    we praise your name and join their unending hymn:

Holy, holy, holy Lord, God of power and might,
heaven and earth are full of your glory.
    Hosanna in the highest.
Blessed is he who comes in the name of the Lord.
    Hosanna in the highest.

Holy are you, and blessed is your Son Jesus Christ.
He leads us into your loving arms.

Your Spirit anointed him
    to preach good news to the poor,
    to proclaim release to the captives and
    recovering of sight to the blind,
    to set at liberty those who are oppressed, and
    to announce that the time had come
    when you would save your people.
He healed the sick, fed the hungry, and ate with sinners.

By the baptism of his suffering, death, and resurrection,
    you gave birth to your church,
    delivered us from slavery to sin and death,
    and made with us a new covenant
    by water and the Spirit.

On the night in which he gave himself up for us
    he took bread, gave thanks to you, broke the bread,
    gave it to his disciples, and said,
"Take, eat; this is my body which is given for you.
Do this in remembrance of me."

When the supper was over he took the cup,
    gave thanks to you, gave it to his disciples, and said,
"Drink from this, all of you; this is my blood of the
    new covenant poured out for you and for many
        for the forgiveness of sins.
Do this as often as you drink it,
    in remembrance of me."

And so, in remembrance of these your mighty acts in Jesus Christ,
we offer ourselves in praise and thanksgiving
    as a holy and living sacrifice,
    in union with Christ's offering for us,
as we proclaim the mystery of faith.

Christ has died; Christ is risen; Christ will come again.

Pour out your Holy Spirit on us gathered here,
    and on these gifts of bread and wine.
Make them be for us the body and blood of Christ,
that we may be for the world the body of Christ,
    redeemed by his blood,
for through him we are born anew.

By your Spirit make us one with Christ,
    one with each other and
    one in ministry to all the world,
until Christ comes in final victory and
    we feast at the heavenly banquet.

Through your Son Jesus Christ,
with the Holy Spirit in your holy church,
all honor and glory is yours, almighty God,
    now and for ever.

Amen.

THE LORD'S PRAYER

And now with the confidence of children of God, let us pray: **Our Father...**

BREAKING THE BREAD

The pastor breaks the bread in silence, or while saying:
Because there is one loaf,
we, who are many, are one body, for we all partake of the one loaf.
The bread which we break is a sharing in the body of Christ.

The pastor lifts the cup in silence, or while saying:
The cup over which we give thanks is a sharing in the blood of Christ.

GIVING THE BREAD AND CUP

The bread and cup are given to the people, with these or other words being exchanged:
The body of Christ, given for you. **Amen.**
The blood of Christ, given for you. **Amen.**

PRAYER AFTER RECEIVING

Eternal God, we give you thanks for this holy mystery
    in which you have given yourself to us.
Help us be a blessing to others
    as we have been blessed by you.
Grant that we may go into the world
    in the strength of your Spirit,
        to give ourselves for others.
in the name of Jesus Christ our Lord.
Amen.

Third Sunday in Lent (a)

Exodus 17:1-7; Psalm 95; Romans 5:1-11; John 4:5-42

The Lord be with you.
And also with you.
Lift up your hearts.
We lift them up to the Lord.
Let us give thanks to the Lord our God.
It is right to give our thanks and praise.

It is right, and a good and joyful thing
    always and everywhere to give thanks to you,
      Almighty God, Creator of heaven and earth.
You led your people through the wilderness
    and filled them with water
        where there was none.

And so, with your people on earth
    and all the company of heaven,
    we praise your name and join their unending hymn:

Holy, holy, holy Lord, God of power and might,
heaven and earth are full of your glory.
    Hosanna in the highest.
Blessed is he who comes in the name of the Lord.
    Hosanna in the highest.

Holy are you, and blessed is your Son Jesus Christ.
He is the living water come down from heaven.
We are reconciled with you
    through his death
      and resurrection.

Your Spirit anointed him
    to preach good news to the poor,
    to proclaim release to the captives and
    recovering of sight to the blind,
    to set at liberty those who are oppressed, and
    to announce that the time had come
    when you would save your people.
He healed the sick, fed the hungry, and ate with sinners.

By the baptism of his suffering, death, and resurrection,
    you gave birth to your church,
    delivered us from slavery to sin and death,
    and made with us a new covenant
    by water and the Spirit.

On the night in which he gave himself up for us
    he took bread, gave thanks to you, broke the bread,
    gave it to his disciples, and said,
"Take, eat; this is my body which is given for you.
Do this in remembrance of me."

When the supper was over he took the cup,
    gave thanks to you, gave it to his disciples, and said,
"Drink from this, all of you; this is my blood of the
    new covenant poured out for you and for many
        for the forgiveness of sins.
Do this as often as you drink it,
    in remembrance of me."

And so, in remembrance of these your mighty acts in Jesus Christ,
we offer ourselves in praise and thanksgiving
    as a holy and living sacrifice,
    in union with Christ's offering for us,
as we proclaim the mystery of faith.

Christ has died; Christ is risen; Christ will come again.

Pour out your Holy Spirit on us gathered here,
    and on these gifts of bread and wine.
Make them be for us the body and blood of Christ,
that we may be for the world the body of Christ,
    redeemed by his blood,
through which we have obtained access to your grace
    and share in the hope of your glory.

By your Spirit make us one with Christ,
    one with each other and
    one in ministry to all the world,
until Christ comes in final victory and
    we feast at the heavenly banquet.

Through your Son Jesus Christ,
with the Holy Spirit in your holy church,
all honor and glory is yours, almighty God,
    now and for ever.

Amen.

THE LORD'S PRAYER

And now with the confidence of children of God, let us pray: **Our Father...**

BREAKING THE BREAD

The pastor breaks the bread in silence, or while saying:
Because there is one loaf,
we, who are many, are one body, for we all partake of the one loaf.
The bread which we break is a sharing in the body of Christ.

The pastor lifts the cup in silence, or while saying:
The cup over which we give thanks is a sharing in the blood of Christ.

GIVING THE BREAD AND CUP

The bread and cup are given to the people, with these or other words being exchanged:
The body of Christ, given for you. **Amen.**
The blood of Christ, given for you. **Amen.**

PRAYER AFTER RECEIVING

Eternal God, we give you thanks for this holy mystery
    in which you have given yourself to us.
If we must suffer for you,
    let it be so,
        that we might grow all the stronger in hope.
Grant that we may go into the world
    in the strength of your Spirit,
    to give ourselves for others.
in the name of Jesus Christ our Lord.
Amen.

Fourth Sunday in Lent (a)

1 Samuel 16:1-13; Psalm 23; Ephesians 5:8-14; John 9:1-41

The Lord be with you.
And also with you.
Lift up your hearts.
We lift them up to the Lord.
Let us give thanks to the Lord our God.
It is right to give our thanks and praise.

It is right, and a good and joyful thing
    always and everywhere to give thanks to you,
    Almighty God, Creator of heaven and earth.
You chose David to lead your people
    and had Samuel anoint him with oil.

And so, with your people on earth
    and all the company of heaven,
    we praise your name and join their unending hymn:

Holy, holy, holy Lord, God of power and might,
heaven and earth are full of your glory.
    Hosanna in the highest.
Blessed is he who comes in the name of the Lord.
    Hosanna in the highest.

Holy are you, and blessed is your Son Jesus Christ.
He showed the world
    that disabilities are not caused by sin,
and all are precious in your eyes.

Your Spirit anointed him
    to preach good news to the poor,
    to proclaim release to the captives and
    recovering of sight to the blind,
    to set at liberty those who are oppressed, and
    to announce that the time had come
    when you would save your people.
He healed the sick, fed the hungry, and ate with sinners.

By the baptism of his suffering, death, and resurrection,
    you gave birth to your church,
    delivered us from slavery to sin and death,
    and made with us a new covenant
    by water and the Spirit.

On the night in which he gave himself up for us
    he took bread, gave thanks to you, broke the bread,
    gave it to his disciples, and said,
"Take, eat; this is my body which is given for you.
Do this in remembrance of me."

When the supper was over he took the cup,
    gave thanks to you, gave it to his disciples, and said,
"Drink from this, all of you; this is my blood of the
    new covenant poured out for you and for many
        for the forgiveness of sins.
Do this as often as you drink it,
    in remembrance of me."

And so, in remembrance of these your mighty acts in Jesus Christ,
we offer ourselves in praise and thanksgiving
    as a holy and living sacrifice,
    in union with Christ's offering for us,
as we proclaim the mystery of faith.

Christ has died; Christ is risen; Christ will come again.

Pour out your Holy Spirit on us gathered here,
    and on these gifts of bread and wine.
Make them be for us the body and blood of Christ,
that we may be for the world the body of Christ,
    redeemed by his blood,
that we might live as children of the light.

By your Spirit make us one with Christ,
    one with each other and
    one in ministry to all the world,
until Christ comes in final victory and
    we feast at the heavenly banquet.

Through your Son Jesus Christ,
with the Holy Spirit in your holy church,
all honor and glory is yours, almighty God,
      now and for ever.

Amen.

THE LORD'S PRAYER

And now with the confidence of children of God, let us pray: **Our Father...**

BREAKING THE BREAD

The pastor breaks the bread in silence, or while saying:
Because there is one loaf,
we, who are many, are one body, for we all partake of the one loaf.
The bread which we break is a sharing in the body of Christ.

The pastor lifts the cup in silence, or while saying:
The cup over which we give thanks is a sharing in the blood of Christ.

GIVING THE BREAD AND CUP

The bread and cup are given to the people, with these or other words being exchanged:
The body of Christ, given for you. **Amen.**
The blood of Christ, given for you. **Amen.**

PRAYER AFTER RECEIVING

Eternal God, we give you thanks for this holy mystery
      in which you have given yourself to us.
Let us be the bearers of your light
      into the dark corners
            of the world.
Grant that we may go into the world
      in the strength of your Spirit,
            to give ourselves for others.
in the name of Jesus Christ our Lord.
Amen.

Fifth Sunday in Lent (a)

Ezekiel 37:1-14; Psalm 130; Romans 8:6-11; John 11:1-45

The Lord be with you.
And also with you.
Lift up your hearts.
We lift them up to the Lord.
Let us give thanks to the Lord our God.
It is right to give our thanks and praise.

It is right, and a good and joyful thing
    always and everywhere to give thanks to you,
    Almighty God, Creator of heaven and earth.
You created all things and called them good.
You gave life to all your creatures
    and breathed your Spirit
        into those who believe.

And so, with your people on earth
    and all the company of heaven,
    we praise your name and join their unending hymn:

Holy, holy, holy Lord, God of power and might,
heaven and earth are full of your glory.
    Hosanna in the highest.
Blessed is he who comes in the name of the Lord.
    Hosanna in the highest.

Holy are you, and blessed is your Son Jesus Christ.
He is the resurrection and the life.
Those who believe in him,
    even though they die, will live.

Your Spirit anointed him
    to preach good news to the poor,
    to proclaim release to the captives and
    recovering of sight to the blind,
    to set at liberty those who are oppressed, and
    to announce that the time had come
    when you would save your people.
He healed the sick, fed the hungry, and ate with sinners.

By the baptism of his suffering, death, and resurrection,
    you gave birth to your church,
    delivered us from slavery to sin and death,
    and made with us a new covenant
    by water and the Spirit.

On the night in which he gave himself up for us
    he took bread, gave thanks to you, broke the bread,
    gave it to his disciples, and said,
"Take, eat; this is my body which is given for you.
Do this in remembrance of me."

When the supper was over he took the cup,
    gave thanks to you, gave it to his disciples, and said,
"Drink from this, all of you; this is my blood of the
    new covenant poured out for you and for many
        for the forgiveness of sins.
Do this as often as you drink it,
    in remembrance of me."

And so, in remembrance of these your mighty acts in Jesus Christ,
we offer ourselves in praise and thanksgiving
    as a holy and living sacrifice,
    in union with Christ's offering for us,
as we proclaim the mystery of faith.

Christ has died; Christ is risen; Christ will come again.

Pour out your Holy Spirit on us gathered here,
    and on these gifts of bread and wine.
Make them be for us the body and blood of Christ,
that we may be for the world the body of Christ,
    redeemed by his blood,
for through it we receive the Spirit
    and where the Spirit is, there is life and peace.

By your Spirit make us one with Christ,
    one with each other and
    one in ministry to all the world,
until Christ comes in final victory and
    we feast at the heavenly banquet.

O'Donnell, *Lift Up Your Hearts 3rd ed. Year A*

Through your Son Jesus Christ,
with the Holy Spirit in your holy church,
all honor and glory is yours, almighty God,
    now and for ever.

Amen.

THE LORD'S PRAYER

And now with the confidence of children of God, let us pray: **Our Father...**

BREAKING THE BREAD

The pastor breaks the bread in silence, or while saying:
Because there is one loaf,
we, who are many, are one body, for we all partake of the one loaf.
The bread which we break is a sharing in the body of Christ.

The pastor lifts the cup in silence, or while saying:
The cup over which we give thanks is a sharing in the blood of Christ.

GIVING THE BREAD AND CUP

The bread and cup are given to the people, with these or other words being exchanged:
The body of Christ, given for you. **Amen.**
The blood of Christ, given for you. **Amen.**

PRAYER AFTER RECEIVING

Eternal God, we give you thanks for this holy mystery
    in which you have given yourself to us.
Through your Spirit we receive life and peace.
Grant that we may go into the world
    in the strength of your Spirit,
        to give ourselves for others.
in the name of Jesus Christ our Lord.
Amen.

Passion/Palm Sunday (a)

Palm: *Matthew 21:1-11; Psalm 119:1-2,19-29.*
Passion: *Isaiah 50:4-9a; Psalm 31:9-16; Philippians 2:5-11; Matthew 26:14-27:66*

The Lord be with you.
And also with you.
Lift up your hearts.
We lift them up to the Lord.
Let us give thanks to the Lord our God.
It is right to give our thanks and praise.

It is right, and a good and joyful thing
    always and everywhere to give thanks to you,
    Almighty God, Creator of heaven and earth.
This is the day which you have made.
Let us rejoice and be glad in it.

And so, with your people on earth
    and all the company of heaven,
    we praise your name and join their unending hymn:

Holy, holy, holy Lord, God of power and might,
heaven and earth are full of your glory.
    Hosanna in the highest.
Blessed is he who comes in the name of the Lord.
    Hosanna in the highest.

Holy are you, and blessed is your Son Jesus Christ,
who, though he was in the form of God,
    emptied himself, taking the form of a slave,
    being born in human form,
he humbled himself and became obedient unto death.

Your Spirit anointed him
    to preach good news to the poor,
    to proclaim release to the captives and
    recovering of sight to the blind,
    to set at liberty those who are oppressed, and
    to announce that the time had come
    when you would save your people.
He healed the sick, fed the hungry, and ate with sinners.

By the baptism of his suffering, death, and resurrection,
　　you gave birth to your church,
　　delivered us from slavery to sin and death,
　　and made with us a new covenant
　　by water and the Spirit.

On the night in which he gave himself up for us
　　he took bread, gave thanks to you, broke the bread,
　　gave it to his disciples, and said,
"Take, eat; this is my body which is given for you.
Do this in remembrance of me."

When the supper was over he took the cup,
　　gave thanks to you, gave it to his disciples, and said,
"Drink from this, all of you; this is my blood of the
　　new covenant poured out for you and for many
　　　　for the forgiveness of sins.
Do this as often as you drink it,
　　in remembrance of me."

And so, in remembrance of these your mighty acts in Jesus Christ,
we offer ourselves in praise and thanksgiving
　　as a holy and living sacrifice,
　　in union with Christ's offering for us,
as we proclaim the mystery of faith.

Christ has died; Christ is risen; Christ will come again.

Pour out your Holy Spirit on us gathered here,
　　and on these gifts of bread and wine.
Make them be for us the body and blood of Christ,
that we may be for the world the body of Christ,
　　redeemed by his blood,
that at his name every knee should bow
　　and every tongue confess that is Jesus Christ is Lord.

By your Spirit make us one with Christ,
　　one with each other and
　　one in ministry to all the world,
until Christ comes in final victory and
　　we feast at the heavenly banquet.

Through your Son Jesus Christ,
with the Holy Spirit in your holy church,
all honor and glory is yours, almighty God,
    now and for ever.

Amen.

THE LORD'S PRAYER
And now with the confidence of children of God, let us pray: **Our Father...**

BREAKING THE BREAD
The pastor breaks the bread in silence, or while saying:
Because there is one loaf,
we, who are many, are one body, for we all partake of the one loaf.
The bread which we break is a sharing in the body of Christ.

The pastor lifts the cup in silence, or while saying:
The cup over which we give thanks is a sharing in the blood of Christ.

GIVING THE BREAD AND CUP
The bread and cup are given to the people, with these or other words being exchanged:
The body of Christ, given for you. **Amen.**
The blood of Christ, given for you. **Amen.**

PRAYER AFTER RECEIVING
Eternal God, we give you thanks for this holy mystery
    in which you have given yourself to us.
Though our flesh may be weak,
    may our spirits be strong.
Grant that we may go into the world
    in the strength of your Spirit,
    to give ourselves for others.
in the name of Jesus Christ our Lord.
Amen.

Monday of Holy Week

Isaiah 42:1-9; Psalm 36:5-11; Hebrews 9:11-15; John 12:1-11

The Lord be with you.
And also with you.
Lift up your hearts.
We lift them up to the Lord.
Let us give thanks to the Lord our God.
It is right to give our thanks and praise.

It is right, and a good and joyful thing
    always and everywhere to give thanks to you,
    Almighty God, Creator of heaven and earth.
You chose your servant to bring forth justice to the nations.
He will not grow faint or be crushed until he has established justice upon the earth.
To you, who created the heavens and stretched them out,
who spread out the earth and what comes from it,
who gives breath to the people upon it and spirit to those who walk in it
we give your our unending praise.

And so, with your people on earth
    and all the company of heaven,
    we praise your name and join their unending hymn:

Holy, holy, holy Lord, God of power and might,
heaven and earth are full of your glory.
    Hosanna in the highest.
Blessed is he who comes in the name of the Lord.
    Hosanna in the highest.

Holy are you, and blessed is your Son Jesus Christ.
He is the high priest of all good things.

Your Spirit anointed him
    to preach good news to the poor,
    to proclaim release to the captives and
    recovering of sight to the blind,
    to set at liberty those who are oppressed, and
    to announce that the time had come
    when you would save your people.
He healed the sick, fed the hungry, and ate with sinners.

By the baptism of his suffering, death, and resurrection,
   you gave birth to your church,
   delivered us from slavery to sin and death,
   and made with us a new covenant
   by water and the Spirit.

On the night in which he gave himself up for us
   he took bread, gave thanks to you, broke the bread,
   gave it to his disciples, and said,
"Take, eat; this is my body which is given for you.
Do this in remembrance of me."

When the supper was over he took the cup,
   gave thanks to you, gave it to his disciples, and said,
"Drink from this, all of you; this is my blood of the
   new covenant poured out for you and for many
      for the forgiveness of sins.
Do this as often as you drink it,
   in remembrance of me."

And so, in remembrance of these your mighty acts in Jesus Christ,
we offer ourselves in praise and thanksgiving
   as a holy and living sacrifice,
   in union with Christ's offering for us,
as we proclaim the mystery of faith.

Christ has died; Christ is risen; Christ will come again.

Pour out your Holy Spirit on us gathered here,
   and on these gifts of bread and wine.
Make them be for us the body and blood of Christ,
that we may be for the world the body of Christ,
   redeemed by his blood,
      through which we receive the promised eternal inheritance.

By your Spirit make us one with Christ,
   one with each other and
   one in ministry to all the world,
until Christ comes in final victory and
   we feast at the heavenly banquet.

Through your Son Jesus Christ,
with the Holy Spirit in your holy church,
all honor and glory is yours, almighty God,
     now and for ever.

Amen.

THE LORD'S PRAYER

And now with the confidence of children of God, let us pray: **Our Father...**

BREAKING THE BREAD

The pastor breaks the bread in silence, or while saying:
Because there is one loaf,
we, who are many, are one body, for we all partake of the one loaf.
The bread which we break is a sharing in the body of Christ.

The pastor lifts the cup in silence, or while saying:
The cup over which we give thanks is a sharing in the blood of Christ.

GIVING THE BREAD AND CUP

The bread and cup are given to the people, with these or other words being exchanged:
The body of Christ, given for you. **Amen.**
The blood of Christ, given for you. **Amen.**

PRAYER AFTER RECEIVING

Eternal God, we give you thanks for this holy mystery
     in which you have given yourself to us.
Comfort us as we enter this most holy of weeks.
Grant that we may go into the world
     in the strength of your Spirit,
     to give ourselves for others.
in the name of Jesus Christ our Lord.
Amen.

Tuesday of Holy Week

Isaiah 49:1-7; Psalm 71:1-14; 1 Corinthians 1:18-31; John 12:20-36

The Lord be with you.
And also with you.
Lift up your hearts.
We lift them up to the Lord.
Let us give thanks to the Lord our God.
It is right to give our thanks and praise.

It is right, and a good and joyful thing
    always and everywhere to give thanks to you,
      Almighty God, Creator of heaven and earth.
You sent your servant to be a light to the nations;
    that salvation might reach to the ends of the earth.
In our human wisdom, he seemed foolish to offer himself for sacrifice.
Yet your foolishness is greater than our wisdom.
Only you knew how the drama must be played out
    for the remission of sins.

And so, with your people on earth
    and all the company of heaven,
      we praise your name and join their unending hymn:

Holy, holy, holy Lord, God of power and might,
heaven and earth are full of your glory.
    Hosanna in the highest.
Blessed is he who comes in the name of the Lord.
    Hosanna in the highest.

Holy are you, and blessed is your Son Jesus Christ.
for through his death we are given life.

Your Spirit anointed him
    to preach good news to the poor,
    to proclaim release to the captives and
    recovering of sight to the blind,
    to set at liberty those who are oppressed, and
    to announce that the time had come
    when you would save your people.
He healed the sick, fed the hungry, and ate with sinners.

By the baptism of his suffering, death, and resurrection,
  you gave birth to your church,
  delivered us from slavery to sin and death,
  and made with us a new covenant
  by water and the Spirit.

On the night in which he gave himself up for us
  he took bread, gave thanks to you, broke the bread,
  gave it to his disciples, and said,
"Take, eat; this is my body which is given for you.
Do this in remembrance of me."

When the supper was over he took the cup,
  gave thanks to you, gave it to his disciples, and said,
"Drink from this, all of you; this is my blood of the
  new covenant poured out for you and for many
    for the forgiveness of sins.
Do this as often as you drink it,
  in remembrance of me."

And so, in remembrance of these your mighty acts in Jesus Christ,
we offer ourselves in praise and thanksgiving
  as a holy and living sacrifice,
  in union with Christ's offering for us,
as we proclaim the mystery of faith.

Christ has died; Christ is risen; Christ will come again.

Pour out your Holy Spirit on us gathered here,
  and on these gifts of bread and wine.
Make them be for us the body and blood of Christ,
that we may be for the world the body of Christ,
  redeemed by his blood,
    the source of our life.

By your Spirit make us one with Christ,
  one with each other and
  one in ministry to all the world,
until Christ comes in final victory and
  we feast at the heavenly banquet.

Through your Son Jesus Christ,
with the Holy Spirit in your holy church,
all honor and glory is yours, almighty God,
    now and for ever.

Amen.

THE LORD'S PRAYER
And now with the confidence of children of God, let us pray: **Our Father...**

BREAKING THE BREAD
The pastor breaks the bread in silence, or while saying:
Because there is one loaf,
we, who are many, are one body, for we all partake of the one loaf.
The bread which we break is a sharing in the body of Christ.

The pastor lifts the cup in silence, or while saying:
The cup over which we give thanks is a sharing in the blood of Christ.

GIVING THE BREAD AND CUP
The bread and cup are given to the people, with these or other words being exchanged:
The body of Christ, given for you. **Amen.**
The blood of Christ, given for you. **Amen.**

PRAYER AFTER RECEIVING

Eternal God, we give you thanks for this holy mystery
    in which you have given yourself to us.
Let your wisdom reign in our hearts.
Grant that we may go into the world
    in the strength of your Spirit,
    to give ourselves for others.
in the name of Jesus Christ our Lord.
Amen.

Isaiah 50:4-9a; Psalm 70; Hebrews 12:1-3; John 13:21-32

The Lord be with you.
And also with you.
Lift up your hearts.
We lift them up to the Lord.
Let us give thanks to the Lord our God.
It is right to give our thanks and praise.

It is right, and a good and joyful thing
    always and everywhere to give thanks to you,
      Almighty God, Creator of heaven and earth.
You have not spared your servant from humiliation,
    but you have vindicated him
        before your throne.

And so, with your people on earth
    and all the company of heaven,
      we praise your name and join their unending hymn:

Holy, holy, holy Lord, God of power and might,
heaven and earth are full of your glory.
    Hosanna in the highest.
Blessed is he who comes in the name of the Lord.
    Hosanna in the highest.

Holy are you, and blessed is your Son Jesus Christ.
He is the pioneer and protector of our faith.
He endured the cross for us,
    disregarding its shame,
and has taken his seat at your right hand.

Your Spirit anointed him
    to preach good news to the poor,
    to proclaim release to the captives and
    recovering of sight to the blind,
    to set at liberty those who are oppressed, and
    to announce that the time had come
    when you would save your people.
He healed the sick, fed the hungry, and ate with sinners.

By the baptism of his suffering, death, and resurrection,
 you gave birth to your church,
 delivered us from slavery to sin and death,
 and made with us a new covenant
 by water and the Spirit.

On the night in which he gave himself up for us
 he took bread, gave thanks to you, broke the bread,
 gave it to his disciples, and said,
"Take, eat; this is my body which is given for you.
Do this in remembrance of me."

When the supper was over he took the cup,
 gave thanks to you, gave it to his disciples, and said,
"Drink from this, all of you; this is my blood of the
 new covenant poured out for you and for many
 for the forgiveness of sins.
Do this as often as you drink it,
 in remembrance of me."

And so, in remembrance of these your mighty acts in Jesus Christ,
we offer ourselves in praise and thanksgiving
 as a holy and living sacrifice,
 in union with Christ's offering for us,
as we proclaim the mystery of faith.

Christ has died; Christ is risen; Christ will come again.

Pour out your Holy Spirit on us gathered here,
 and on these gifts of bread and wine.
Make them be for us the body and blood of Christ,
that we may be for the world the body of Christ,
 redeemed by his blood,
that we might set aside the weight of sin
 that clings so closely to us.

By your Spirit make us one with Christ,
 one with each other and
 one in ministry to all the world,
until Christ comes in final victory and
 we feast at the heavenly banquet.

O'Donnell, *Lift Up Your Hearts 3rd ed. Year A*

Through your Son Jesus Christ,
with the Holy Spirit in your holy church,
all honor and glory is yours, almighty God,
    now and for ever.

Amen.

THE LORD'S PRAYER

And now with the confidence of children of God, let us pray: **Our Father...**

BREAKING THE BREAD

The pastor breaks the bread in silence, or while saying:
Because there is one loaf,
we, who are many, are one body, for we all partake of the one loaf.
The bread which we break is a sharing in the body of Christ.

The pastor lifts the cup in silence, or while saying:
The cup over which we give thanks is a sharing in the blood of Christ.

GIVING THE BREAD AND CUP

The bread and cup are given to the people, with these or other words being exchanged:
The body of Christ, given for you. **Amen.**
The blood of Christ, given for you. **Amen.**

PRAYER AFTER RECEIVING

Eternal God, we give you thanks for this holy mystery
    in which you have given yourself to us.
Empower us to run with perseverance
    the race that is set before us.
Grant that we may go into the world
    in the strength of your Spirit,
        to give ourselves for others.
in the name of Jesus Christ our Lord.
Amen.

Holy (Maundy) Thursday

Exodus 12:1-4, (5-10), 11-14; Psalm 116:1-2, 12-19; 1 Corinthians 11:23-26; John 13:1-17, 31b-35

The Lord be with you.
And also with you.
Lift up your hearts.
We lift them up to the Lord.
Let us give thanks to the Lord our God.
It is right to give our thanks and praise.

It is right, and a good and joyful thing
    always and everywhere to give thanks to you,
      Almighty God, Creator of heaven and earth.
You spared your people
    with the blood of lambs
      smeared over their doorposts.
And the angel of death passed over them and spared them.

And so, with your people on earth
    and all the company of heaven,
    we praise your name and join their unending hymn:

Holy, holy, holy Lord, God of power and might,
heaven and earth are full of your glory.
    Hosanna in the highest.
Blessed is he who comes in the name of the Lord.
    Hosanna in the highest.

Holy are you, and blessed is your Son Jesus Christ.
He is our Passover Lamb.
He was betrayed and sacrificed for the forgiveness of our sins.
He gave us a new commandment to love one another.

Your Spirit anointed him
    to preach good news to the poor,
    to proclaim release to the captives and
    recovering of sight to the blind,
    to set at liberty those who are oppressed, and
    to announce that the time had come
    when you would save your people.
He healed the sick, fed the hungry, and ate with sinners.

By the baptism of his suffering, death, and resurrection,
    you gave birth to your church,
    delivered us from slavery to sin and death,
    and made with us a new covenant
    by water and the Spirit.

On the night in which he gave himself up for us
    he took bread, gave thanks to you, broke the bread,
    gave it to his disciples, and said,
"Take, eat; this is my body which is given for you.
Do this in remembrance of me."

When the supper was over he took the cup,
    gave thanks to you, gave it to his disciples, and said,
"Drink from this, all of you; this is my blood of the
    new covenant poured out for you and for many
        for the forgiveness of sins.
Do this as often as you drink it,
    in remembrance of me."

And so, in remembrance of these your mighty acts in Jesus Christ,
we offer ourselves in praise and thanksgiving
    as a holy and living sacrifice,
    in union with Christ's offering for us,
as we proclaim the mystery of faith.

Christ has died; Christ is risen; Christ will come again.

Pour out your Holy Spirit on us gathered here,
    and on these gifts of bread and wine.
Make them be for us the body and blood of Christ,
that we may be for the world the body of Christ,
    redeemed by his blood
for when we show love to one another,
    all will know that we are his disciples.

By your Spirit make us one with Christ,
    one with each other and
    one in ministry to all the world,
until Christ comes in final victory and
    we feast at the heavenly banquet.

Through your Son Jesus Christ,
with the Holy Spirit in your holy church,
all honor and glory is yours, almighty God,
    now and for ever.

Amen.

THE LORD'S PRAYER

And now with the confidence of children of God, let us pray: **Our Father...**

BREAKING THE BREAD

The pastor breaks the bread in silence, or while saying:
Because there is one loaf,
we, who are many, are one body, for we all partake of the one loaf.
The bread which we break is a sharing in the body of Christ.

The pastor lifts the cup in silence, or while saying:
The cup over which we give thanks is a sharing in the blood of Christ.

GIVING THE BREAD AND CUP

The bread and cup are given to the people, with these or other words being exchanged:
The body of Christ, given for you. **Amen.**
The blood of Christ, given for you. **Amen.**

PRAYER AFTER RECEIVING

Eternal God, we give you thanks for this holy mystery
    in which you have given yourself to us.
Empowered by this sacrament,
grant that we may go into the world
    in the strength of your Spirit,
      to give ourselves for others.
in the name of Jesus Christ our Lord.
Amen.

The Lord be with you.
And also with you.
Lift up your hearts.
We lift them up to the Lord.
Let us give thanks to the Lord our God.
It is right to give our thanks and praise.

It is right, and a good and joyful thing
    always and everywhere to give thanks to you,
    Almighty God, Creator of heaven and earth.
You made all things and called them good.
You made us in your own image,
    but we disobeyed and drew away from you.
    allowing sin to rule our lives and actions.
You have remained steadfast in your love for us
    and draw us back to you.

And so, with your people on earth
    and all the company of heaven,
    we praise your name and join their unending hymn:

Holy, holy, holy Lord, God of power and might,
heaven and earth are full of your glory.
    Hosanna in the highest.
Blessed is he who comes in the name of the Lord.
    Hosanna in the highest.

Holy are you, and blessed is your Son Jesus Christ.
He came to wash away the stain of sin from us
    by offering himself up on our behalf.

Your Spirit anointed him
    to preach good news to the poor,
    to proclaim release to the captives and
    recovering of sight to the blind,
    to set at liberty those who are oppressed, and
    to announce that the time had come
    when you would save your people.
He healed the sick, fed the hungry, and ate with sinners.

By the baptism of his suffering, death, and resurrection,
   you gave birth to your church,
   delivered us from slavery to sin and death,
   and made with us a new covenant
   by water and the Spirit.

On the night in which he gave himself up for us
   he took bread, gave thanks to you, broke the bread,
   gave it to his disciples, and said,
"Take, eat; this is my body which is given for you.
Do this in remembrance of me."

When the supper was over he took the cup,
   gave thanks to you, gave it to his disciples, and said,
"Drink from this, all of you; this is my blood of the
   new covenant poured out for you and for many
      for the forgiveness of sins.
Do this as often as you drink it,
   in remembrance of me."

And so, in remembrance of these your mighty acts in Jesus Christ,
we offer ourselves in praise and thanksgiving
   as a holy and living sacrifice,
   in union with Christ's offering for us,
as we proclaim the mystery of faith.

Christ has died; Christ is risen; Christ will come again.

Pour out your Holy Spirit on us gathered here,
   and on these gifts of bread and wine.
Make them be for us the body and blood of Christ,
that we may be for the world the body of Christ,
   redeemed by his blood,
for we are dead to sin and alive to God in Christ Jesus.

By your Spirit make us one with Christ,
   one with each other and
   one in ministry to all the world,
until Christ comes in final victory and
   we feast at the heavenly banquet.

Through your Son Jesus Christ,
with the Holy Spirit in your holy church,
all honor and glory is yours, almighty God,
    now and for ever.

Amen.

THE LORD'S PRAYER
And now with the confidence of children of God, let us pray: **Our Father...**

BREAKING THE BREAD
The pastor breaks the bread in silence, or while saying:
Because there is one loaf,
we, who are many, are one body, for we all partake of the one loaf.
The bread which we break is a sharing in the body of Christ.

The pastor lifts the cup in silence, or while saying:
The cup over which we give thanks is a sharing in the blood of Christ.

GIVING THE BREAD AND CUP
The bread and cup are given to the people, with these or other words being exchanged:
The body of Christ, given for you. **Amen.**
The blood of Christ, given for you. **Amen.**

PRAYER AFTER RECEIVING
Eternal God, we give you thanks for this holy mystery
    in which you have given yourself to us.
Through our baptism we are a resurrection people.
Grant that we may go into the world
    in the strength of your Spirit,
    to give ourselves for others.
in the name of Jesus Christ our Lord.
Amen.

Easter Day (a)

Acts 10:34-43; Psalm 118:1-2, 14-24; Colossians 3:1-4; John 20:1-18 or Matthew 28:1-10

The Lord be with you.
And also with you.
Lift up your hearts.
We lift them up to the Lord.
Let us give thanks to the Lord our God.
It is right to give our thanks and praise.

It is right, and a good and joyful thing
     always and everywhere to give thanks to you,
     Almighty God, Creator of heaven and earth.
You show no partiality,
     but accept everyone who fears you
          and does what is right in faith.

And so, with your people on earth
     and all the company of heaven,
     we praise your name and join their unending hymn:

Holy, holy, holy Lord, God of power and might,
heaven and earth are full of your glory.
     Hosanna in the highest.
Blessed is he who comes in the name of the Lord.
     Hosanna in the highest.

Holy are you, and blessed is your Son Jesus Christ.
You raised him from the dead,
     revealing him first to Mary Magdalene
          and then to the disciples.

Your Spirit anointed him
     to preach good news to the poor,
     to proclaim release to the captives and
     recovering of sight to the blind,
     to set at liberty those who are oppressed, and
     to announce that the time had come
     when you would save your people.
He healed the sick, fed the hungry, and ate with sinners.

By the baptism of his suffering, death, and resurrection,
    you gave birth to your church,
    delivered us from slavery to sin and death,
    and made with us a new covenant
    by water and the Spirit.

On the night in which he gave himself up for us
    he took bread, gave thanks to you, broke the bread,
    gave it to his disciples, and said,
"Take, eat; this is my body which is given for you.
Do this in remembrance of me."

When the supper was over he took the cup,
    gave thanks to you, gave it to his disciples, and said,
"Drink from this, all of you; this is my blood of the
    new covenant poured out for you and for many
        for the forgiveness of sins.
Do this as often as you drink it,
    in remembrance of me."

And so, in remembrance of these your mighty acts in Jesus Christ,
we offer ourselves in praise and thanksgiving
    as a holy and living sacrifice,
    in union with Christ's offering for us,
as we proclaim the mystery of faith.

Christ has died; Christ is risen; Christ will come again.

Pour out your Holy Spirit on us gathered here,
    and on these gifts of bread and wine.
Make them be for us the body and blood of Christ,
that we may be for the world the body of Christ,
    redeemed by his blood,
that we might set our minds
    on the things that are above.

By your Spirit make us one with Christ,
    one with each other and
    one in ministry to all the world,
until Christ comes in final victory and
    we feast at the heavenly banquet.

Through your Son Jesus Christ,
with the Holy Spirit in your holy church,
all honor and glory is yours, almighty God,
    now and for ever.

Amen.

THE LORD'S PRAYER
And now with the confidence of children of God, let us pray: **Our Father...**

BREAKING THE BREAD
The pastor breaks the bread in silence, or while saying:
Because there is one loaf,
we, who are many, are one body, for we all partake of the one loaf.
The bread which we break is a sharing in the body of Christ.

The pastor lifts the cup in silence, or while saying:
The cup over which we give thanks is a sharing in the blood of Christ.

GIVING THE BREAD AND CUP
The bread and cup are given to the people, with these or other words being exchanged:
The body of Christ, given for you. **Amen.**
The blood of Christ, given for you. **Amen.**

PRAYER AFTER RECEIVING
Eternal God, we give you thanks for this holy mystery
    in which you have given yourself to us.
Empower us to spread
    through word and deed
that everyone who believes in him
    receives forgiveness of their sins.
Grant that we may go into the world
    in the strength of your Spirit,
    to give ourselves for others.
in the name of Jesus Christ our Lord.
Amen.

Second Sunday of Easter (a)

Acts 2:14a, 22-32; Psalm 16; 1 Peter 1:3-9; John 20:19-31

The Lord be with you.
And also with you.
Lift up your hearts.
We lift them up to the Lord.
Let us give thanks to the Lord our God.
It is right to give our thanks and praise.

It is right, and a good and joyful thing
    always and everywhere to give thanks to you,
    Almighty God, Creator of heaven and earth.
By your great mercy you have given us new birth
    into a living hope through the resurrection
        of Jesus Christ from the dead.

And so, with your people on earth
    and all the company of heaven,
    we praise your name and join their unending hymn:

Holy, holy, holy Lord, God of power and might,
heaven and earth are full of your glory.
    Hosanna in the highest.
Blessed is he who comes in the name of the Lord.
    Hosanna in the highest.

Holy are you, and blessed is your Son Jesus Christ.
Although we have not seen him, we love him.
Even though we do not see him now,
    we believe in him
        with an indescribable and glorious joy.

Your Spirit anointed him
    to preach good news to the poor,
    to proclaim release to the captives and
    recovering of sight to the blind,
    to set at liberty those who are oppressed, and
    to announce that the time had come
    when you would save your people.
He healed the sick, fed the hungry, and ate with sinners.

By the baptism of his suffering, death, and resurrection,
    you gave birth to your church,
    delivered us from slavery to sin and death,
    and made with us a new covenant
    by water and the Spirit.

On the night in which he gave himself up for us
    he took bread, gave thanks to you, broke the bread,
    gave it to his disciples, and said,
"Take, eat; this is my body which is given for you.
Do this in remembrance of me."

When the supper was over he took the cup,
    gave thanks to you, gave it to his disciples, and said,
"Drink from this, all of you; this is my blood of the
    new covenant poured out for you and for many
        for the forgiveness of sins.
Do this as often as you drink it,
    in remembrance of me."

And so, in remembrance of these your mighty acts in Jesus Christ,
we offer ourselves in praise and thanksgiving
    as a holy and living sacrifice,
    in union with Christ's offering for us,
as we proclaim the mystery of faith.

Christ has died; Christ is risen; Christ will come again.

Pour out your Holy Spirit on us gathered here,
    and on these gifts of bread and wine.
Make them be for us the body and blood of Christ,
that we may be for the world the body of Christ,
    redeemed by his blood,
through him we receive the outcome of our faith,
    the salvation of our souls.

By your Spirit make us one with Christ,
    one with each other and
    one in ministry to all the world,
until Christ comes in final victory and
    we feast at the heavenly banquet.

Through your Son Jesus Christ,
with the Holy Spirit in your holy church,
all honor and glory is yours, almighty God,
    now and for ever.

Amen.

THE LORD'S PRAYER

And now with the confidence of children of God, let us pray: **Our Father...**

BREAKING THE BREAD

The pastor breaks the bread in silence, or while saying:
Because there is one loaf,
we, who are many, are one body, for we all partake of the one loaf.
The bread which we break is a sharing in the body of Christ.

The pastor lifts the cup in silence, or while saying:
The cup over which we give thanks is a sharing in the blood of Christ.

GIVING THE BREAD AND CUP

The bread and cup are given to the people, with these or other words being exchanged:
The body of Christ, given for you. **Amen.**
The blood of Christ, given for you. **Amen.**

PRAYER AFTER RECEIVING

Eternal God, we give you thanks for this holy mystery
    in which you have given yourself to us.
For as God sent Jesus to us,
    Jesus sends us.
Grant that we may go into the world
    in the strength of your Spirit,
    to give ourselves for others.
in the name of Jesus Christ our Lord.
Amen.

Third Sunday of Easter (a)

Acts 2:14a, 36-41; Psalm 116:1-4, 12-19; 1 Peter 1:17-23; Luke 24:13-35

The Lord be with you.
And also with you.
Lift up your hearts.
We lift them up to the Lord.
Let us give thanks to the Lord our God.
It is right to give our thanks and praise.

It is right, and a good and joyful thing
    always and everywhere to give thanks to you,
    Almighty God, Creator of heaven and earth.
You saved your people through your Son Jesus,
    who is both Lord and Messiah;
        that all who repent in his name are forgiven.

And so, with your people on earth
    and all the company of heaven,
    we praise your name and join their unending hymn:

Holy, holy, holy Lord, God of power and might,
heaven and earth are full of your glory.
    Hosanna in the highest.
Blessed is he who comes in the name of the Lord.
    Hosanna in the highest.

Holy are you, and blessed is your Son Jesus Christ.
He was destined
    before the foundation of the world;
but is revealed now for our sake.

Your Spirit anointed him
    to preach good news to the poor,
    to proclaim release to the captives and
    recovering of sight to the blind,
    to set at liberty those who are oppressed, and
    to announce that the time had come
    when you would save your people.
He healed the sick, fed the hungry, and ate with sinners.

By the baptism of his suffering, death, and resurrection,
  you gave birth to your church,
    delivered us from slavery to sin and death,
    and made with us a new covenant
    by water and the Spirit.

On the night in which he gave himself up for us
    he took bread, gave thanks to you, broke the bread,
    gave it to his disciples, and said,
"Take, eat; this is my body which is given for you.
Do this in remembrance of me."

When the supper was over he took the cup,
    gave thanks to you, gave it to his disciples, and said,
"Drink from this, all of you; this is my blood of the
    new covenant poured out for you and for many
        for the forgiveness of sins.
Do this as often as you drink it,
    in remembrance of me."

And so, in remembrance of these your mighty acts in Jesus Christ,
we offer ourselves in praise and thanksgiving
    as a holy and living sacrifice,
    in union with Christ's offering for us,
as we proclaim the mystery of faith.

Christ has died; Christ is risen; Christ will come again.

Pour out your Holy Spirit on us gathered here,
    and on these gifts of bread and wine.
Make them be for us the body and blood of Christ,
that we may be for the world the body of Christ,
    redeemed by his blood,
for we have been born anew
    through your living and enduring word.

By your Spirit make us one with Christ,
    one with each other and
    one in ministry to all the world,
until Christ comes in final victory and
    we feast at the heavenly banquet.

Through your Son Jesus Christ,
with the Holy Spirit in your holy church,
all honor and glory is yours, almighty God,
     now and for ever.

Amen.

THE LORD'S PRAYER

And now with the confidence of children of God, let us pray: **Our Father…**

BREAKING THE BREAD

The pastor breaks the bread in silence, or while saying:
Because there is one loaf,
we, who are many, are one body, for we all partake of the one loaf.
The bread which we break is a sharing in the body of Christ.

The pastor lifts the cup in silence, or while saying:
The cup over which we give thanks is a sharing in the blood of Christ.

GIVING THE BREAD AND CUP

The bread and cup are given to the people, with these or other words being exchanged:
The body of Christ, given for you. **Amen.**
The blood of Christ, given for you. **Amen.**

PRAYER AFTER RECEIVING

Eternal God, we give you thanks for this holy mystery
     in which you have given yourself to us.
May our hearts burn within
     as we encounter the Risen Christ in our lives.
Grant that we may go into the world
     in the strength of your Spirit,
     to give ourselves for others.
in the name of Jesus Christ our Lord.
Amen.

Fourth Sunday of Easter (a)

Acts 2:42-47; Psalm 23; 1 Peter 2:19-25; John 10:1-10

The Lord be with you.
And also with you.
Lift up your hearts.
We lift them up to the Lord.
Let us give thanks to the Lord our God.
It is right to give our thanks and praise.

It is right, and a good and joyful thing
    always and everywhere to give thanks to you,
    Almighty God, Creator of heaven and earth.
You sent Jesus to bear our sins
    that we might be free
        and live in righteousness.

And so, with your people on earth
    and all the company of heaven,
    we praise your name and join their unending hymn:

Holy, holy, holy Lord, God of power and might,
heaven and earth are full of your glory.
    Hosanna in the highest.
Blessed is he who comes in the name of the Lord.
    Hosanna in the highest.

Holy are you, and blessed is your Son Jesus Christ.
He committed no sin, and no deceit.
He was abused, but did not return abuse.
When he suffered, he did not threaten;
    but entrusted himself to you who judges justly.

Your Spirit anointed him
    to preach good news to the poor,
    to proclaim release to the captives and
    recovering of sight to the blind,
    to set at liberty those who are oppressed, and
    to announce that the time had come
    when you would save your people.
He healed the sick, fed the hungry, and ate with sinners.

By the baptism of his suffering, death, and resurrection,
    you gave birth to your church,
    delivered us from slavery to sin and death,
    and made with us a new covenant
    by water and the Spirit.

On the night in which he gave himself up for us
    he took bread, gave thanks to you, broke the bread,
    gave it to his disciples, and said,
"Take, eat; this is my body which is given for you.
Do this in remembrance of me."

When the supper was over he took the cup,
    gave thanks to you, gave it to his disciples, and said,
"Drink from this, all of you; this is my blood of the
    new covenant poured out for you and for many
        for the forgiveness of sins.
Do this as often as you drink it,
    in remembrance of me."

And so, in remembrance of these your mighty acts in Jesus Christ,
we offer ourselves in praise and thanksgiving
    as a holy and living sacrifice,
    in union with Christ's offering for us,
as we proclaim the mystery of faith.

Christ has died; Christ is risen; Christ will come again.

Pour out your Holy Spirit on us gathered here,
    and on these gifts of bread and wine.
Make them be for us the body and blood of Christ,
that we may be for the world the body of Christ,
    redeemed by his blood,
for by his wounds we are healed.

By your Spirit make us one with Christ,
    one with each other and
    one in ministry to all the world,
until Christ comes in final victory and
    we feast at the heavenly banquet.

Through your Son Jesus Christ,
with the Holy Spirit in your holy church,
all honor and glory is yours, almighty God,
    now and for ever.

Amen.

THE LORD'S PRAYER

And now with the confidence of children of God, let us pray: **Our Father...**

BREAKING THE BREAD

The pastor breaks the bread in silence, or while saying:
Because there is one loaf,
we, who are many, are one body, for we all partake of the one loaf.
The bread which we break is a sharing in the body of Christ.

The pastor lifts the cup in silence, or while saying:
The cup over which we give thanks is a sharing in the blood of Christ.

GIVING THE BREAD AND CUP

The bread and cup are given to the people, with these or other words being exchanged:
The body of Christ, given for you. **Amen.**
The blood of Christ, given for you. **Amen.**

PRAYER AFTER RECEIVING

Eternal God, we give you thanks for this holy mystery
    in which you have given yourself to us.
In times of difficulty,
    turn us toward the shepherd
        and guardian of our souls.
Grant that we may go into the world
    in the strength of your Spirit,
    to give ourselves for others.
in the name of Jesus Christ our Lord.
Amen.

Fifth Sunday of Easter (a)

Acts 7:55-60; Psalm 31:1-5; 15-16; 1 Peter 2:2-10; John 14:1-14

The Lord be with you.
And also with you.
Lift up your hearts.
We lift them up to the Lord.
Let us give thanks to the Lord our God.
It is right to give our thanks and praise.

It is right, and a good and joyful thing
    always and everywhere to give thanks to you,
      Almighty God, Creator of heaven and earth.
You are our rock and our fortress;
    our refuge in times of peril.
Your steadfast love has saved us from our enemies.

And so, with your people on earth
    and all the company of heaven,
      we praise your name and join their unending hymn:

Holy, holy, holy Lord, God of power and might,
heaven and earth are full of your glory.
    Hosanna in the highest.
Blessed is he who comes in the name of the Lord.
    Hosanna in the highest.

Holy are you, and blessed is your Son Jesus Christ.
He is your chosen and precious cornerstone
    upon which you are building your spiritual house
      here on earth.

Your Spirit anointed him
    to preach good news to the poor,
    to proclaim release to the captives and
    recovering of sight to the blind,
    to set at liberty those who are oppressed, and
    to announce that the time had come
    when you would save your people.
He healed the sick, fed the hungry, and ate with sinners.

By the baptism of his suffering, death, and resurrection,
  you gave birth to your church,
  delivered us from slavery to sin and death,
  and made with us a new covenant
  by water and the Spirit.

On the night in which he gave himself up for us
  he took bread, gave thanks to you, broke the bread,
  gave it to his disciples, and said,
"Take, eat; this is my body which is given for you.
Do this in remembrance of me."

When the supper was over he took the cup,
  gave thanks to you, gave it to his disciples, and said,
"Drink from this, all of you; this is my blood of the
  new covenant poured out for you and for many
    for the forgiveness of sins.
Do this as often as you drink it,
  in remembrance of me."

And so, in remembrance of these your mighty acts in Jesus Christ,
we offer ourselves in praise and thanksgiving
  as a holy and living sacrifice,
  in union with Christ's offering for us,
as we proclaim the mystery of faith.

Christ has died; Christ is risen; Christ will come again.

Pour out your Holy Spirit on us gathered here,
  and on these gifts of bread and wine.
Make them be for us the body and blood of Christ,
that we may be for the world the body of Christ,
  redeemed by his blood,
for you have called us out of the darkness
  and into the light.

By your Spirit make us one with Christ,
  one with each other and
  one in ministry to all the world,
until Christ comes in final victory and
  we feast at the heavenly banquet.

Through your Son Jesus Christ,
with the Holy Spirit in your holy church,
all honor and glory is yours, almighty God,
    now and for ever.

Amen.

THE LORD'S PRAYER

And now with the confidence of children of God, let us pray: **Our Father...**

BREAKING THE BREAD

The pastor breaks the bread in silence, or while saying:
Because there is one loaf,
we, who are many, are one body, for we all partake of the one loaf.
The bread which we break is a sharing in the body of Christ.

The pastor lifts the cup in silence, or while saying:
The cup over which we give thanks is a sharing in the blood of Christ.

GIVING THE BREAD AND CUP

The bread and cup are given to the people, with these or other words being exchanged:
The body of Christ, given for you. **Amen.**
The blood of Christ, given for you. **Amen.**

PRAYER AFTER RECEIVING

Eternal God, we give you thanks for this holy mystery
    in which you have given yourself to us.
We know that whatever we ask
    in Jesus name,
        you will do.
Grant that we may go into the world
    in the strength of your Spirit,
    to give ourselves for others.
in the name of Jesus Christ our Lord.
Amen.

Acts 17:22-31; Psalm 66:8-20; 1 Peter 3:13-22; John 14:15-21

The Lord be with you.
And also with you.
Lift up your hearts.
We lift them up to the Lord.
Let us give thanks to the Lord our God.
It is right to give our thanks and praise.

It is right, and a good and joyful thing
    always and everywhere to give thanks to you,
    Almighty God, Creator of heaven and earth.
You are the One God
    above all gods.
In you we live and move
    and have our being.

And so, with your people on earth
    and all the company of heaven,
    we praise your name and join their unending hymn:

Holy, holy, holy Lord, God of power and might,
heaven and earth are full of your glory.
    Hosanna in the highest.
Blessed is he who comes in the name of the Lord.
    Hosanna in the highest.

Holy are you, and blessed is your Son Jesus Christ.
He suffered and died for our sins once for all,
    for the righteous and the unrighteous,
        in order to bring all people to You.

Your Spirit anointed him
    to preach good news to the poor,
    to proclaim release to the captives and
    recovering of sight to the blind,
    to set at liberty those who are oppressed, and
    to announce that the time had come
    when you would save your people.
He healed the sick, fed the hungry, and ate with sinners.

By the baptism of his suffering, death, and resurrection,
  you gave birth to your church,
  delivered us from slavery to sin and death,
  and made with us a new covenant
  by water and the Spirit.

On the night in which he gave himself up for us
  he took bread, gave thanks to you, broke the bread,
  gave it to his disciples, and said,
"Take, eat; this is my body which is given for you.
Do this in remembrance of me."

When the supper was over he took the cup,
  gave thanks to you, gave it to his disciples, and said,
"Drink from this, all of you; this is my blood of the
  new covenant poured out for you and for many
    for the forgiveness of sins.
Do this as often as you drink it,
  in remembrance of me."

And so, in remembrance of these your mighty acts in Jesus Christ,
we offer ourselves in praise and thanksgiving
  as a holy and living sacrifice,
  in union with Christ's offering for us,
as we proclaim the mystery of faith.

Christ has died; Christ is risen; Christ will come again.

Pour out your Holy Spirit on us gathered here,
  and on these gifts of bread and wine.
Make them be for us the body and blood of Christ,
that we may be for the world the body of Christ,
  redeemed by his blood,
for in our hearts we sanctify Christ as Lord.

By your Spirit make us one with Christ,
  one with each other and
  one in ministry to all the world,
until Christ comes in final victory and
  we feast at the heavenly banquet.

Through your Son Jesus Christ,
with the Holy Spirit in your holy church,
all honor and glory is yours, almighty God,
     now and for ever.

Amen.

THE LORD'S PRAYER

And now with the confidence of children of God, let us pray: **Our Father...**

BREAKING THE BREAD

The pastor breaks the bread in silence, or while saying:
Because there is one loaf,
we, who are many, are one body, for we all partake of the one loaf.
The bread which we break is a sharing in the body of Christ.

The pastor lifts the cup in silence, or while saying:
The cup over which we give thanks is a sharing in the blood of Christ.

GIVING THE BREAD AND CUP

The bread and cup are given to the people, with these or other words being exchanged:
The body of Christ, given for you. **Amen.**
The blood of Christ, given for you. **Amen.**

PRAYER AFTER RECEIVING

Eternal God, we give you thanks for this holy mystery
     in which you have given yourself to us.
Open our hearts
     to receive the Spirit of truth.
Grant that we may go into the world
     in the strength of your Spirit,
     to give ourselves for others.
in the name of Jesus Christ our Lord.
Amen.

Ascension of the Lord

Acts 1:1-11; Psalm 47; Ephesians 1:15-23; Luke 24:44-53

The Lord be with you.
And also with you.
Lift up your hearts.
We lift them up to the Lord.
Let us give thanks to the Lord our God.
It is right to give our thanks and praise.

It is right, and a good and joyful thing
    always and everywhere to give thanks to you,
    Almighty God, Creator of heaven and earth.
You have given us the spirit of wisdom and revelation
    so that, with the eye of our hearts enlightened,
    we might know the hope to which you have called us.

And so, with your people on earth
    and all the company of heaven,
    we praise your name and join their unending hymn:

Holy, holy, holy Lord, God of power and might,
heaven and earth are full of your glory.
    Hosanna in the highest.
Blessed is he who comes in the name of the Lord.
    Hosanna in the highest.

Holy are you, and blessed is your Son Jesus Christ.
You put your power to work in him
    when you raised him from the dead.
He ascended into heaven
    and is seated at your right hand.

Your Spirit anointed him
    to preach good news to the poor,
    to proclaim release to the captives and
    recovering of sight to the blind,
    to set at liberty those who are oppressed, and
    to announce that the time had come
    when you would save your people.
He healed the sick, fed the hungry, and ate with sinners.

By the baptism of his suffering, death, and resurrection,
    you gave birth to your church,
    delivered us from slavery to sin and death,
    and made with us a new covenant
    by water and the Spirit.

On the night in which he gave himself up for us
    he took bread, gave thanks to you, broke the bread,
    gave it to his disciples, and said,
"Take, eat; this is my body which is given for you.
Do this in remembrance of me."

When the supper was over he took the cup,
    gave thanks to you, gave it to his disciples, and said,
"Drink from this, all of you; this is my blood of the
    new covenant poured out for you and for many
        for the forgiveness of sins.
Do this as often as you drink it,
    in remembrance of me."

And so, in remembrance of these your mighty acts in Jesus Christ,
we offer ourselves in praise and thanksgiving
    as a holy and living sacrifice,
    in union with Christ's offering for us,
as we proclaim the mystery of faith.

Christ has died; Christ is risen; Christ will come again.

Pour out your Holy Spirit on us gathered here,
    and on these gifts of bread and wine.
Make them be for us the body and blood of Christ,
that we may be for the world the body of Christ,
    redeemed by his blood,
for you have put all things under his feet
    and have made him head over all things for his church.

By your Spirit make us one with Christ,
    one with each other and
    one in ministry to all the world,
until Christ comes in final victory and
    we feast at the heavenly banquet.

Through your Son Jesus Christ,
with the Holy Spirit in your holy church,
all honor and glory is yours, almighty God,
    now and for ever.

Amen.

THE LORD'S PRAYER

And now with the confidence of children of God, let us pray: **Our Father...**

BREAKING THE BREAD

The pastor breaks the bread in silence, or while saying:
Because there is one loaf,
we, who are many, are one body, for we all partake of the one loaf.
The bread which we break is a sharing in the body of Christ.

The pastor lifts the cup in silence, or while saying:
The cup over which we give thanks is a sharing in the blood of Christ.

GIVING THE BREAD AND CUP

The bread and cup are given to the people, with these or other words being exchanged:
The body of Christ, given for you. **Amen.**
The blood of Christ, given for you. **Amen.**

PRAYER AFTER RECEIVING

Eternal God, we give you thanks for this holy mystery
    in which you have given yourself to us.
Empower us to be the body of Christ here on earth.
Grant that we may go into the world
    in the strength of your Spirit,
    to give ourselves for others.
in the name of Jesus Christ our Lord.
Amen.

Seventh Sunday of Easter (a)

Acts 1:6-14; Psalm 68:1-10, 32-35; 1 Peter 4:12-14, 5:6-11; John 17:1-11

The Lord be with you.
And also with you.
Lift up your hearts.
We lift them up to the Lord.
Let us give thanks to the Lord our God.
It is right to give our thanks and praise.

It is right, and a good and joyful thing
    always and everywhere to give thanks to you,
      Almighty God, Creator of heaven and earth.
We cast our anxieties upon you;
    for your love for us
        is beyond measure.

And so, with your people on earth
    and all the company of heaven,
    we praise your name and join their unending hymn:

Holy, holy, holy Lord, God of power and might,
heaven and earth are full of your glory.
    Hosanna in the highest.
Blessed is he who comes in the name of the Lord.
    Hosanna in the highest.

Holy are you, and blessed is your Son Jesus Christ.
You have given him authority over all people,
    to give eternal life
        to all whom you have given him.

Your Spirit anointed him
    to preach good news to the poor,
    to proclaim release to the captives and
    recovering of sight to the blind,
    to set at liberty those who are oppressed, and
    to announce that the time had come
    when you would save your people.
He healed the sick, fed the hungry, and ate with sinners.

By the baptism of his suffering, death, and resurrection,
    you gave birth to your church,
    delivered us from slavery to sin and death,
    and made with us a new covenant
    by water and the Spirit.

On the night in which he gave himself up for us
    he took bread, gave thanks to you, broke the bread,
    gave it to his disciples, and said,
"Take, eat; this is my body which is given for you.
Do this in remembrance of me."

When the supper was over he took the cup,
    gave thanks to you, gave it to his disciples, and said,
"Drink from this, all of you; this is my blood of the
    new covenant poured out for you and for many
        for the forgiveness of sins.
Do this as often as you drink it,
    in remembrance of me."

And so, in remembrance of these your mighty acts in Jesus Christ,
we offer ourselves in praise and thanksgiving
    as a holy and living sacrifice,
    in union with Christ's offering for us,
as we proclaim the mystery of faith.

Christ has died; Christ is risen; Christ will come again.

Pour out your Holy Spirit on us gathered here,
    and on these gifts of bread and wine.
Make them be for us the body and blood of Christ,
that we may be for the world the body of Christ,
    redeemed by his blood.
May they empower us to resist evil
    and to hold steadfast in our faith.

By your Spirit make us one with Christ,
    one with each other and
    one in ministry to all the world,
until Christ comes in final victory and
    we feast at the heavenly banquet.

Through your Son Jesus Christ,
with the Holy Spirit in your holy church,
all honor and glory is yours, almighty God,
    now and for ever.

Amen.

THE LORD'S PRAYER

And now with the confidence of children of God, let us pray: **Our Father...**

BREAKING THE BREAD

The pastor breaks the bread in silence, or while saying:
Because there is one loaf,
we, who are many, are one body, for we all partake of the one loaf.
The bread which we break is a sharing in the body of Christ.

The pastor lifts the cup in silence, or while saying:
The cup over which we give thanks is a sharing in the blood of Christ.

GIVING THE BREAD AND CUP

The bread and cup are given to the people, with these or other words being exchanged:
The body of Christ, given for you. **Amen.**
The blood of Christ, given for you. **Amen.**

PRAYER AFTER RECEIVING

Eternal God, we give you thanks for this holy mystery
    in which you have given yourself to us.
Grant that we accept
    whatever sufferings come our way
        that are a result of our steadfast faith.
Grant that we may go into the world
    in the strength of your Spirit,
    to give ourselves for others.
in the name of Jesus Christ our Lord.
Amen.

Day of Pentecost (a)

Acts 2:1-21; Psalm 104:24-34, 35b; 1 Corinthians 12:3b-13; John 7:37-39

The Lord be with you.
And also with you.
Lift up your hearts.
We lift them up to the Lord.
Let us give thanks to the Lord our God.
It is right to give our thanks and praise.

It is right, and a good and joyful thing
    always and everywhere to give thanks to you,
    Almighty God, Creator of heaven and earth.
You sent forth your Spirit
    and all creation rejoices.
May your glory endure forever.
We will sing to you as long as we live;
    we will sing to you as long as we have being.

And so, with your people on earth
    and all the company of heaven,
    we praise your name and join their unending hymn:

Holy, holy, holy Lord, God of power and might,
heaven and earth are full of your glory.
    Hosanna in the highest.
Blessed is he who comes in the name of the Lord.
    Hosanna in the highest.

Holy are you, and blessed is your Son Jesus Christ.
    who lived and died
        that we might inherit your Spirit.

Your Spirit anointed him
    to preach good news to the poor,
    to proclaim release to the captives and
    recovering of sight to the blind,
    to set at liberty those who are oppressed, and
    to announce that the time had come
    when you would save your people.
He healed the sick, fed the hungry, and ate with sinners.

By the baptism of his suffering, death, and resurrection,
    you gave birth to your church,
    delivered us from slavery to sin and death,
    and made with us a new covenant
    by water and the Spirit.

On the night in which he gave himself up for us
    he took bread, gave thanks to you, broke the bread,
    gave it to his disciples, and said,
"Take, eat; this is my body which is given for you.
Do this in remembrance of me."

When the supper was over he took the cup,
    gave thanks to you, gave it to his disciples, and said,
"Drink from this, all of you; this is my blood of the
    new covenant poured out for you and for many
        for the forgiveness of sins.
Do this as often as you drink it,
    in remembrance of me."

And so, in remembrance of these your mighty acts in Jesus Christ,
we offer ourselves in praise and thanksgiving
    as a holy and living sacrifice,
    in union with Christ's offering for us,
as we proclaim the mystery of faith.

Christ has died; Christ is risen; Christ will come again.

Pour out your Holy Spirit on us gathered here,
    and on these gifts of bread and wine.
Make them be for us the body and blood of Christ,
that we may be for the world the body of Christ,
    redeemed by his blood
that we too might receive the Spirit
    and be empowered to go forth as you call us to do.

By your Spirit make us one with Christ,
    one with each other and
    one in ministry to all the world,
until Christ comes in final victory and
    we feast at the heavenly banquet.

Through your Son Jesus Christ,
with the Holy Spirit in your holy church,
all honor and glory is yours, almighty God,
   now and for ever.

Amen.

THE LORD'S PRAYER
And now with the confidence of children of God, let us pray: **Our Father...**

BREAKING THE BREAD
The pastor breaks the bread in silence, or while saying:
Because there is one loaf,
we, who are many, are one body, for we all partake of the one loaf.
The bread which we break is a sharing in the body of Christ.

The pastor lifts the cup in silence, or while saying:
The cup over which we give thanks is a sharing in the blood of Christ.

GIVING THE BREAD AND CUP
The bread and cup are given to the people, with these or other words being exchanged:
The body of Christ, given for you. **Amen.**
The blood of Christ, given for you. **Amen.**

PRAYER AFTER RECEIVING
Eternal God, we give you thanks for this holy mystery
   in which you have given yourself to us.
Touch us with your Spirit
   and ignite our hearts with faith and power.
Grant that we may go into the world
   in the strength of your Spirit,
   to give ourselves for others.
in the name of Jesus Christ our Lord.
Amen.

Trinity Sunday (a)

Genesis 1:1-2:4a; Psalm 8; 2 Corinthians 13:11-13; Matthew 28:16-20

The Lord be with you.
And also with you.
Lift up your hearts.
We lift them up to the Lord.
Let us give thanks to the Lord our God.
It is right to give our thanks and praise.

It is right, and a good and joyful thing
    always and everywhere to give thanks to you,
    Almighty God, Creator of heaven and earth.
You brought order out of chaos,
    making all creatures and plants,
        sun and moon and stars.
You created human beings
    in your own image
and declared that all you had created was good.

And so, with your people on earth
    and all the company of heaven,
    we praise your name and join their unending hymn:

Holy, holy, holy Lord, God of power and might,
heaven and earth are full of your glory.
    Hosanna in the highest.
Blessed is he who comes in the name of the Lord.
    Hosanna in the highest.

Holy are you, and blessed is your Son Jesus Christ.
You have given him all authority in heaven and on earth.

Your Spirit anointed him
    to preach good news to the poor,
    to proclaim release to the captives and
    recovering of sight to the blind,
    to set at liberty those who are oppressed, and
    to announce that the time had come
    when you would save your people.
He healed the sick, fed the hungry, and ate with sinners.

By the baptism of his suffering, death, and resurrection,
    you gave birth to your church,
    delivered us from slavery to sin and death,
    and made with us a new covenant
    by water and the Spirit.

On the night in which he gave himself up for us
    he took bread, gave thanks to you, broke the bread,
    gave it to his disciples, and said,
"Take, eat; this is my body which is given for you.
Do this in remembrance of me."

When the supper was over he took the cup,
    gave thanks to you, gave it to his disciples, and said,
"Drink from this, all of you; this is my blood of the
    new covenant poured out for you and for many
        for the forgiveness of sins.
Do this as often as you drink it,
    in remembrance of me."

And so, in remembrance of these your mighty acts in Jesus Christ,
we offer ourselves in praise and thanksgiving
    as a holy and living sacrifice,
    in union with Christ's offering for us,
as we proclaim the mystery of faith.

Christ has died; Christ is risen; Christ will come again.

Pour out your Holy Spirit on us gathered here,
    and on these gifts of bread and wine.
Make them be for us the body and blood of Christ,
that we may be for the world the body of Christ,
  redeemed by his blood,
that all people everywhere
    might know his saving love.

By your Spirit make us one with Christ,
    one with each other and
    one in ministry to all the world,
until Christ comes in final victory and
    we feast at the heavenly banquet.

Through your Son Jesus Christ,
with the Holy Spirit in your holy church,
all honor and glory is yours, almighty God,
    now and for ever.

Amen.

THE LORD'S PRAYER
And now with the confidence of children of God, let us pray: **Our Father...**

BREAKING THE BREAD
The pastor breaks the bread in silence, or while saying:
Because there is one loaf,
we, who are many, are one body, for we all partake of the one loaf.
The bread which we break is a sharing in the body of Christ.

The pastor lifts the cup in silence, or while saying:
The cup over which we give thanks is a sharing in the blood of Christ.

GIVING THE BREAD AND CUP
The bread and cup are given to the people, with these or other words being exchanged:
The body of Christ, given for you. **Amen.**
The blood of Christ, given for you. **Amen.**

PRAYER AFTER RECEIVING
Eternal God, we give you thanks for this holy mystery
    in which you have given yourself to us.
We honor you as Father, Son, and Holy Spirit.
Grant that we may go into the world
    in the strength of your Spirit,
        to give ourselves for others.
in the name of Jesus Christ our Lord.
Amen.

Genesis 6:11-22, 7:24, 8:14-19; Psalm 46; Romans 1:16-17, 3:22b-28 (29-31);
Matthew 7:21-29

The Lord be with you.
And also with you.
Lift up your hearts.
We lift them up to the Lord.
Let us give thanks to the Lord our God.
It is right to give our thanks and praise.

It is right, and a good and joyful thing
 always and everywhere to give thanks to you,
  Almighty God, Creator of heaven and earth.
When you saw the world was steeped in sin
 you washed it clean with water
  and made a new covenant with Noah.

And so, with your people on earth
 and all the company of heaven,
 we praise your name and join their unending hymn:

Holy, holy, holy Lord, God of power and might,
heaven and earth are full of your glory.
 Hosanna in the highest.
Blessed is he who comes in the name of the Lord.
 Hosanna in the highest.

Holy are you, and blessed is your Son Jesus Christ.
Through him we are justified
 and receive the gift of grace.

Your Spirit anointed him
 to preach good news to the poor,
 to proclaim release to the captives and
 recovering of sight to the blind,
 to set at liberty those who are oppressed, and
 to announce that the time had come
 when you would save your people.
He healed the sick, fed the hungry, and ate with sinners.

By the baptism of his suffering, death, and resurrection,
    you gave birth to your church,
    delivered us from slavery to sin and death,
    and made with us a new covenant
    by water and the Spirit.

On the night in which he gave himself up for us
    he took bread, gave thanks to you, broke the bread,
    gave it to his disciples, and said,
"Take, eat; this is my body which is given for you.
Do this in remembrance of me."

When the supper was over he took the cup,
    gave thanks to you, gave it to his disciples, and said,
"Drink from this, all of you; this is my blood of the
    new covenant poured out for you and for many
        for the forgiveness of sins.
Do this as often as you drink it,
    in remembrance of me."

And so, in remembrance of these your mighty acts in Jesus Christ,
we offer ourselves in praise and thanksgiving
    as a holy and living sacrifice,
    in union with Christ's offering for us,
as we proclaim the mystery of faith.

Christ has died; Christ is risen; Christ will come again.

Pour out your Holy Spirit on us gathered here,
    and on these gifts of bread and wine.
Make them be for us the body and blood of Christ,
    redeemed by his blood,
that all might hear his words
    and act wisely on them.

By your Spirit make us one with Christ,
    one with each other and
    one in ministry to all the world,
until Christ comes in final victory and
    we feast at the heavenly banquet.

Through your Son Jesus Christ,
with the Holy Spirit in your holy church,
all honor and glory is yours, almighty God,
     now and for ever.

Amen.

THE LORD'S PRAYER

And now with the confidence of children of God, let us pray: **Our Father...**

BREAKING THE BREAD

The pastor breaks the bread in silence, or while saying:
Because there is one loaf,
we, who are many, are one body, for we all partake of the one loaf.
The bread which we break is a sharing in the body of Christ.

The pastor lifts the cup in silence, or while saying:
The cup over which we give thanks is a sharing in the blood of Christ.

GIVING THE BREAD AND CUP

The bread and cup are given to the people, with these or other words being exchanged:
The body of Christ, given for you. **Amen.**
The blood of Christ, given for you. **Amen.**

PRAYER AFTER RECEIVING

Eternal God, we give you thanks for this holy mystery
     in which you have given yourself to us.
Let us be instruments of your grace.
Grant that we may go into the world
     in the strength of your Spirit,
          to give ourselves for others.
in the name of Jesus Christ our Lord.
Amen.

Genesis 12:1-9; Psalm 33:1-12; Romans 4:13-25; Matthew 9:9-13, 18-26

The Lord be with you.
And also with you.
Lift up your hearts.
We lift them up to the Lord.
Let us give thanks to the Lord our God.
It is right to give our thanks and praise.

It is right, and a good and joyful thing
    always and everywhere to give thanks to you,
        Almighty God, Creator of heaven and earth.
You are the author of life
    and call into existence
        things that did not exist.

And so, with your people on earth
    and all the company of heaven,
    we praise your name and join their unending hymn:

Holy, holy, holy Lord, God of power and might,
heaven and earth are full of your glory.
    Hosanna in the highest.
Blessed is he who comes in the name of the Lord.
    Hosanna in the highest.

Holy are you, and blessed is your Son Jesus Christ.
He came to call sinners
    back to you.

Your Spirit anointed him
    to preach good news to the poor,
    to proclaim release to the captives and
    recovering of sight to the blind,
    to set at liberty those who are oppressed, and
    to announce that the time had come
    when you would save your people.
He healed the sick, fed the hungry, and ate with sinners.

By the baptism of his suffering, death, and resurrection,
    you gave birth to your church,
    delivered us from slavery to sin and death,
    and made with us a new covenant
    by water and the Spirit.

On the night in which he gave himself up for us
    he took bread, gave thanks to you, broke the bread,
    gave it to his disciples, and said,
"Take, eat; this is my body which is given for you.
Do this in remembrance of me."

When the supper was over he took the cup,
    gave thanks to you, gave it to his disciples, and said,
"Drink from this, all of you; this is my blood of the
    new covenant poured out for you and for many
        for the forgiveness of sins.
Do this as often as you drink it,
    in remembrance of me."

And so, in remembrance of these your mighty acts in Jesus Christ,
we offer ourselves in praise and thanksgiving
    as a holy and living sacrifice,
    in union with Christ's offering for us,
as we proclaim the mystery of faith.

Christ has died; Christ is risen; Christ will come again.

Pour out your Holy Spirit on us gathered here,
    and on these gifts of bread and wine.
Make them be for us the body and blood of Christ,
that we may be for the world the body of Christ,
    redeemed by his blood,
and cleansed from all unrighteousness.

By your Spirit make us one with Christ,
    one with each other and
    one in ministry to all the world,
until Christ comes in final victory and
    we feast at the heavenly banquet.

Through your Son Jesus Christ,
with the Holy Spirit in your holy church,
all honor and glory is yours, almighty God,
    now and for ever.

Amen.

THE LORD'S PRAYER

And now with the confidence of children of God, let us pray: **Our Father...**

BREAKING THE BREAD

The pastor breaks the bread in silence, or while saying:
Because there is one loaf,
we, who are many, are one body, for we all partake of the one loaf.
The bread which we break is a sharing in the body of Christ.

The pastor lifts the cup in silence, or while saying:
The cup over which we give thanks is a sharing in the blood of Christ.

GIVING THE BREAD AND CUP

The bread and cup are given to the people, with these or other words being exchanged:
The body of Christ, given for you. **Amen.**
The blood of Christ, given for you. **Amen.**

PRAYER AFTER RECEIVING

Eternal God, we give you thanks for this holy mystery
    in which you have given yourself to us.
You have called us into new life.
Grant that we may go into the world
    in the strength of your Spirit,
        to give ourselves for others.
in the name of Jesus Christ our Lord.
Amen.

The Lord be with you.
And also with you.
Lift up your hearts.
We lift them up to the Lord.
Let us give thanks to the Lord our God.
It is right to give our thanks and praise.

It is right, and a good and joyful thing
    always and everywhere to give thanks to you,
      Almighty God, Creator of heaven and earth.
Nothing is too wonderful for you.
Every blessing comes
    in its due season.

And so, with your people on earth
    and all the company of heaven,
      we praise your name and join their unending hymn:

Holy, holy, holy Lord, God of power and might,
heaven and earth are full of your glory.
    Hosanna in the highest.
Blessed is he who comes in the name of the Lord.
    Hosanna in the highest.

Holy are you, and blessed is your Son Jesus Christ.
He died for us
    while we were yet sinners.
That proves your great love for us.

Your Spirit anointed him
    to preach good news to the poor,
    to proclaim release to the captives and
    recovering of sight to the blind,
    to set at liberty those who are oppressed, and
    to announce that the time had come
    when you would save your people.
He healed the sick, fed the hungry, and ate with sinners.

By the baptism of his suffering, death, and resurrection,
    you gave birth to your church,
    delivered us from slavery to sin and death,
    and made with us a new covenant
    by water and the Spirit.

On the night in which he gave himself up for us
    he took bread, gave thanks to you, broke the bread,
    gave it to his disciples, and said,
"Take, eat; this is my body which is given for you.
Do this in remembrance of me."

When the supper was over he took the cup,
    gave thanks to you, gave it to his disciples, and said,
"Drink from this, all of you; this is my blood of the
    new covenant poured out for you and for many
        for the forgiveness of sins.
Do this as often as you drink it,
    in remembrance of me."

And so, in remembrance of these your mighty acts in Jesus Christ,
we offer ourselves in praise and thanksgiving
    as a holy and living sacrifice,
    in union with Christ's offering for us,
as we proclaim the mystery of faith.

Christ has died; Christ is risen; Christ will come again.

Pour out your Holy Spirit on us gathered here,
    and on these gifts of bread and wine.
Make them be for us the body and blood of Christ,
that we may be for the world the body of Christ,
    redeemed by his blood,
and saved from the wrath to come.

By your Spirit make us one with Christ,
    one with each other and
    one in ministry to all the world,
until Christ comes in final victory and
    we feast at the heavenly banquet.

Through your Son Jesus Christ,
with the Holy Spirit in your holy church,
all honor and glory is yours, almighty God,
    now and for ever.

Amen.

THE LORD'S PRAYER
And now with the confidence of children of God, let us pray: **Our Father...**

BREAKING THE BREAD
The pastor breaks the bread in silence, or while saying:
Because there is one loaf,
we, who are many, are one body, for we all partake of the one loaf.
The bread which we break is a sharing in the body of Christ.

The pastor lifts the cup in silence, or while saying:
The cup over which we give thanks is a sharing in the blood of Christ.

GIVING THE BREAD AND CUP
The bread and cup are given to the people, with these or other words being exchanged:
The body of Christ, given for you. **Amen.**
The blood of Christ, given for you. **Amen.**

PRAYER AFTER RECEIVING
Eternal God, we give you thanks for this holy mystery
    in which you have given yourself to us.
May we be worthy laborers
    for the harvest.
Grant that we may go into the world
    in the strength of your Spirit,
    to give ourselves for others.
in the name of Jesus Christ our Lord.
Amen.

Genesis 21:8-21; Psalm 86:1-10, 16-17 or Psalm 17; Romans 6:1b-11; Matthew 10:24-39

The Lord be with you.
And also with you.
Lift up your hearts.
We lift them up to the Lord.
Let us give thanks to the Lord our God.
It is right to give our thanks and praise.

It is right, and a good and joyful thing
    always and everywhere to give thanks to you,
    Almighty God, Creator of heaven and earth.
You have made all things
    and love all that you have made
      even the lowly sparrow.
How much more you love us.

And so, with your people on earth
    and all the company of heaven,
    we praise your name and join their unending hymn:

Holy, holy, holy Lord, God of power and might,
heaven and earth are full of your glory.
    Hosanna in the highest.
Blessed is he who comes in the name of the Lord.
    Hosanna in the highest.

Holy are you, and blessed is your Son Jesus Christ.
The death he died, he died to sin,
    once for all.
The life he lives, he lives to you.

Your Spirit anointed him
    to preach good news to the poor,
    to proclaim release to the captives and
    recovering of sight to the blind,
    to set at liberty those who are oppressed, and
    to announce that the time had come
    when you would save your people.
He healed the sick, fed the hungry, and ate with sinners.

By the baptism of his suffering, death, and resurrection,
     you gave birth to your church,
     delivered us from slavery to sin and death,
     and made with us a new covenant
     by water and the Spirit.

On the night in which he gave himself up for us
     he took bread, gave thanks to you, broke the bread,
     gave it to his disciples, and said,
"Take, eat; this is my body which is given for you.
Do this in remembrance of me."

When the supper was over he took the cup,
     gave thanks to you, gave it to his disciples, and said,
"Drink from this, all of you; this is my blood of the
     new covenant poured out for you and for many
          for the forgiveness of sins.
Do this as often as you drink it,
     in remembrance of me."

And so, in remembrance of these your mighty acts in Jesus Christ,
we offer ourselves in praise and thanksgiving
     as a holy and living sacrifice,
     in union with Christ's offering for us,
as we proclaim the mystery of faith.

Christ has died; Christ is risen; Christ will come again.

Pour out your Holy Spirit on us gathered here,
     and on these gifts of bread and wine.
Make them be for us the body and blood of Christ,
that we may be for the world the body of Christ,
     redeemed by his blood,
that we might be alive to you
     through him.

By your Spirit make us one with Christ,
     one with each other and
     one in ministry to all the world,
until Christ comes in final victory and
     we feast at the heavenly banquet.

Through your Son Jesus Christ,
with the Holy Spirit in your holy church,
all honor and glory is yours, almighty God,
    now and for ever.

Amen.

THE LORD'S PRAYER

And now with the confidence of children of God, let us pray: **Our Father...**

BREAKING THE BREAD

The pastor breaks the bread in silence, or while saying:
Because there is one loaf,
we, who are many, are one body, for we all partake of the one loaf.
The bread which we break is a sharing in the body of Christ.

The pastor lifts the cup in silence, or while saying:
The cup over which we give thanks is a sharing in the blood of Christ.

GIVING THE BREAD AND CUP

The bread and cup are given to the people, with these or other words being exchanged:
The body of Christ, given for you. **Amen.**
The blood of Christ, given for you. **Amen.**

PRAYER AFTER RECEIVING

Eternal God, we give you thanks for this holy mystery
    in which you have given yourself to us.
We promise never to deny Jesus
    by our thoughts, our words or our deeds.
Grant that we may go into the world
    in the strength of your Spirit,
    to give ourselves for others.
in the name of Jesus Christ our Lord.
Amen.

Genesis 22:1-14; Psalm 13; Romans 6:12-23; Matthew 10:40-42

The Lord be with you.
And also with you.
Lift up your hearts.
We lift them up to the Lord.
Let us give thanks to the Lord our God.
It is right to give our thanks and praise.

It is right, and a good and joyful thing
    always and everywhere to give thanks to you,
    Almighty God, Creator of heaven and earth.
Abraham trusted you enough
    to offer his son Isaac,
        the heir of your promise.
He proved his faithfulness to you
    and you spared his son.

And so, with your people on earth
    and all the company of heaven,
    we praise your name and join their unending hymn:

Holy, holy, holy Lord, God of power and might,
heaven and earth are full of your glory.
    Hosanna in the highest.
Blessed is he who comes in the name of the Lord.
    Hosanna in the highest.

Holy are you, and blessed is your Son Jesus Christ.
Your own son you did not spare;
    his death became the sacrifice for our sins.

Your Spirit anointed him
    to preach good news to the poor,
    to proclaim release to the captives and
    recovering of sight to the blind,
    to set at liberty those who are oppressed, and
    to announce that the time had come
    when you would save your people.
He healed the sick, fed the hungry, and ate with sinners.

By the baptism of his suffering, death, and resurrection,
   you gave birth to your church,
   delivered us from slavery to sin and death,
   and made with us a new covenant
   by water and the Spirit.

On the night in which he gave himself up for us
   he took bread, gave thanks to you, broke the bread,
   gave it to his disciples, and said,
"Take, eat; this is my body which is given for you.
Do this in remembrance of me."

When the supper was over he took the cup,
   gave thanks to you, gave it to his disciples, and said,
"Drink from this, all of you; this is my blood of the
   new covenant poured out for you and for many
      for the forgiveness of sins.
Do this as often as you drink it,
   in remembrance of me."

And so, in remembrance of these your mighty acts in Jesus Christ,
we offer ourselves in praise and thanksgiving
   as a holy and living sacrifice,
   in union with Christ's offering for us,
as we proclaim the mystery of faith.

Christ has died; Christ is risen; Christ will come again.

Pour out your Holy Spirit on us gathered here,
   and on these gifts of bread and wine.
Make them be for us the body and blood of Christ,
that we may be for the world the body of Christ,
   redeemed by his blood,
for we have been set free from sin
   and have become slaves of righteousness.

By your Spirit make us one with Christ,
   one with each other and
   one in ministry to all the world,
until Christ comes in final victory and
   we feast at the heavenly banquet.

Through your Son Jesus Christ,
with the Holy Spirit in your holy church,
all honor and glory is yours, almighty God,
    now and for ever.

Amen.

THE LORD'S PRAYER
And now with the confidence of children of God, let us pray: **Our Father...**

BREAKING THE BREAD
The pastor breaks the bread in silence, or while saying:
Because there is one loaf,
we, who are many, are one body, for we all partake of the one loaf.
The bread which we break is a sharing in the body of Christ.

The pastor lifts the cup in silence, or while saying:
The cup over which we give thanks is a sharing in the blood of Christ.

GIVING THE BREAD AND CUP
The bread and cup are given to the people, with these or other words being exchanged:
The body of Christ, given for you. **Amen.**
The blood of Christ, given for you. **Amen.**

PRAYER AFTER RECEIVING
Eternal God, we give you thanks for this holy mystery
    in which you have given yourself to us.
Helps us welcome
    each person we meet
        as we would welcome Christ.
Grant that we may go into the world
    in the strength of your Spirit,
    to give ourselves for others.
in the name of Jesus Christ our Lord.
Amen.

Proper 9 [July 3-9] (a)

Genesis 24:34-38, 42-49, 58-67; Psalm 45:10-17 or Psalm 72; Romans 7:15-25a; Matthew 11:16-19, 25-30

The Lord be with you.
And also with you.
Lift up your hearts.
We lift them up to the Lord.
Let us give thanks to the Lord our God.
It is right to give our thanks and praise.

It is right, and a good and joyful thing
 always and everywhere to give thanks to you,
 Almighty God, Creator of heaven and earth.
Your true nature, Love, was demonstrated
 when you brought together Isaac and Rebekah.
We delight in your love.

And so, with your people on earth
 and all the company of heaven,
 we praise your name and join their unending hymn:

Holy, holy, holy Lord, God of power and might,
heaven and earth are full of your glory.
 Hosanna in the highest.
Blessed is he who comes in the name of the Lord.
 Hosanna in the highest.

Holy are you, and blessed is your Son Jesus Christ.
When the world was filled with sin,
 you sent him to lead us back to you.
But many resisted him and condemned him to death.

Your Spirit anointed him
 to preach good news to the poor,
 to proclaim release to the captives and
 recovering of sight to the blind,
 to set at liberty those who are oppressed, and
 to announce that the time had come
 when you would save your people.
He healed the sick, fed the hungry, and ate with sinners.

By the baptism of his suffering, death, and resurrection,
 you gave birth to your church,
 delivered us from slavery to sin and death,
 and made with us a new covenant
 by water and the Spirit.

On the night in which he gave himself up for us
 he took bread, gave thanks to you, broke the bread,
 gave it to his disciples, and said,
"Take, eat; this is my body which is given for you.
Do this in remembrance of me."

When the supper was over he took the cup,
 gave thanks to you, gave it to his disciples, and said,
"Drink from this, all of you; this is my blood of the
 new covenant poured out for you and for many
 for the forgiveness of sins.
Do this as often as you drink it,
 in remembrance of me."

And so, in remembrance of these your mighty acts in Jesus Christ,
we offer ourselves in praise and thanksgiving
 as a holy and living sacrifice,
 in union with Christ's offering for us,
as we proclaim the mystery of faith.

Christ has died; Christ is risen; Christ will come again.

Pour out your Holy Spirit on us gathered here,
 and on these gifts of bread and wine.
Make them be for us the body and blood of Christ,
that we may be for the world the body of Christ,
 redeemed by his blood,
for the world is weary and heavily burdened,
 and Christ offers rest for our souls.

By your Spirit make us one with Christ,
 one with each other and
 one in ministry to all the world,
until Christ comes in final victory and
 we feast at the heavenly banquet.

Through your Son Jesus Christ,
with the Holy Spirit in your holy church,
all honor and glory is yours, almighty God,
    now and for ever.

Amen.

THE LORD'S PRAYER
And now with the confidence of children of God, let us pray: **Our Father…**

BREAKING THE BREAD
The pastor breaks the bread in silence, or while saying:
Because there is one loaf,
we, who are many, are one body, for we all partake of the one loaf.
The bread which we break is a sharing in the body of Christ.

The pastor lifts the cup in silence, or while saying:
The cup over which we give thanks is a sharing in the blood of Christ.

GIVING THE BREAD AND CUP
The bread and cup are given to the people, with these or other words being exchanged:
The body of Christ, given for you. **Amen.**
The blood of Christ, given for you. **Amen.**

PRAYER AFTER RECEIVING
Eternal God, we give you thanks for this holy mystery
    in which you have given yourself to us.
Let us rest our burdens
    on the Resurrected Christ.
Grant that we may go into the world
    in the strength of your Spirit,
        to give ourselves for others.
in the name of Jesus Christ our Lord.
Amen.

The Lord be with you.
And also with you.
Lift up your hearts.
We lift them up to the Lord.
Let us give thanks to the Lord our God.
It is right to give our thanks and praise.

It is right, and a good and joyful thing
    always and everywhere to give thanks to you,
       Almighty God, Creator of heaven and earth.
You sow you seeds among all the people,
    but many do not grown in faith; they wither and die.
Blessed are those who take root and grow,
    for the harvest is bountiful.

And so, with your people on earth
    and all the company of heaven,
    we praise your name and join their unending hymn:

Holy, holy, holy Lord, God of power and might,
heaven and earth are full of your glory.
    Hosanna in the highest.
Blessed is he who comes in the name of the Lord.
    Hosanna in the highest.

Holy are you, and blessed is your Son Jesus Christ.
In him is not condemnation,
    for the law of the Spirit sets us free
       from the law of sin.

Your Spirit anointed him
    to preach good news to the poor,
    to proclaim release to the captives and
    recovering of sight to the blind,
    to set at liberty those who are oppressed, and
    to announce that the time had come
    when you would save your people.
He healed the sick, fed the hungry, and ate with sinners.

By the baptism of his suffering, death, and resurrection,
    you gave birth to your church,
    delivered us from slavery to sin and death,
    and made with us a new covenant
    by water and the Spirit.

On the night in which he gave himself up for us
    he took bread, gave thanks to you, broke the bread,
    gave it to his disciples, and said,
"Take, eat; this is my body which is given for you.
Do this in remembrance of me."

When the supper was over he took the cup,
    gave thanks to you, gave it to his disciples, and said,
"Drink from this, all of you; this is my blood of the
    new covenant poured out for you and for many
        for the forgiveness of sins.
Do this as often as you drink it,
    in remembrance of me."

And so, in remembrance of these your mighty acts in Jesus Christ,
we offer ourselves in praise and thanksgiving
    as a holy and living sacrifice,
    in union with Christ's offering for us,
as we proclaim the mystery of faith.

Christ has died; Christ is risen; Christ will come again.

Pour out your Holy Spirit on us gathered here,
    and on these gifts of bread and wine.
Make them be for us the body and blood of Christ,
that we may be for the world the body of Christ,
    redeemed by his blood,
for his spirit lives in us.

By your Spirit make us one with Christ,
    one with each other and
    one in ministry to all the world,
until Christ comes in final victory and
    we feast at the heavenly banquet.

Through your Son Jesus Christ,
with the Holy Spirit in your holy church,
all honor and glory is yours, almighty God,
    now and for ever.

Amen.

THE LORD'S PRAYER
And now with the confidence of children of God, let us pray: **Our Father...**

BREAKING THE BREAD
The pastor breaks the bread in silence, or while saying:
Because there is one loaf,
we, who are many, are one body, for we all partake of the one loaf.
The bread which we break is a sharing in the body of Christ.

The pastor lifts the cup in silence, or while saying:
The cup over which we give thanks is a sharing in the blood of Christ.

GIVING THE BREAD AND CUP
The bread and cup are given to the people, with these or other words being exchanged:
The body of Christ, given for you. **Amen.**
The blood of Christ, given for you. **Amen.**

PRAYER AFTER RECEIVING
Eternal God, we give you thanks for this holy mystery
    in which you have given yourself to us.
May we take root and grow in faith
    that we might bear much fruit.
Grant that we may go into the world
    in the strength of your Spirit,
        to give ourselves for others.
in the name of Jesus Christ our Lord.
Amen.

PROPER 11 [July 17-23] (a)

Genesis 28:10-19a; Psalm 139:1-12, 23-24 or Psalm 86:11-17; Romans 8:12-25; Matthew 13:24-30, 36-43

The Lord be with you.
And also with you.
Lift up your hearts.
We lift them up to the Lord.
Let us give thanks to the Lord our God.
It is right to give our thanks and praise.

It is right, and a good and joyful thing
    always and everywhere to give thanks to you,
    Almighty God, Creator of heaven and earth.
All creation waits with eager longing
    for the revealing of your children,
that it might be freed of decay
    and obtain the glory of your being.

And so, with your people on earth
    and all the company of heaven,
    we praise your name and join their unending hymn:

Holy, holy, holy Lord, God of power and might,
heaven and earth are full of your glory.
    Hosanna in the highest.
Blessed is he who comes in the name of the Lord.
    Hosanna in the highest.

Holy are you, and blessed is your Son Jesus Christ.
He has planted good seed,
    while the evil one has mixed bad seed with it
        to destroy the crop of righteousness.

Your Spirit anointed Jesus
    to preach good news to the poor,
    to proclaim release to the captives and
    recovering of sight to the blind,
    to set at liberty those who are oppressed, and
    to announce that the time had come
    when you would save your people.

He healed the sick, fed the hungry, and ate with sinners.
By the baptism of his suffering, death, and resurrection,
    you gave birth to your church,
    delivered us from slavery to sin and death,
    and made with us a new covenant
    by water and the Spirit.

On the night in which he gave himself up for us
    he took bread, gave thanks to you, broke the bread,
    gave it to his disciples, and said,
"Take, eat; this is my body which is given for you.
Do this in remembrance of me."

When the supper was over he took the cup,
    gave thanks to you, gave it to his disciples, and said,
"Drink from this, all of you; this is my blood of the
    new covenant poured out for you and for many
        for the forgiveness of sins.
Do this as often as you drink it,
    in remembrance of me."

And so, in remembrance of these your mighty acts in Jesus Christ,
we offer ourselves in praise and thanksgiving
    as a holy and living sacrifice,
    in union with Christ's offering for us,
as we proclaim the mystery of faith.

Christ has died; Christ is risen; Christ will come again.

Pour out your Holy Spirit on us gathered here,
    and on these gifts of bread and wine.
Make them be for us the body and blood of Christ,
that we may be for the world the body of Christ,
    redeemed by his blood,
that we might be led by the Spirit in all things.

By your Spirit make us one with Christ,
    one with each other and
    one in ministry to all the world,
until Christ comes in final victory and
    we feast at the heavenly banquet.

Through your Son Jesus Christ,
with the Holy Spirit in your holy church,
all honor and glory is yours, almighty God,
    now and for ever.

Amen.

The Lord's Prayer

And now with the confidence of children of God, let us pray: **Our Father...**

Breaking the Bread

The pastor breaks the bread in silence, or while saying:
Because there is one loaf,
we, who are many, are one body, for we all partake of the one loaf.
The bread which we break is a sharing in the body of Christ.

The pastor lifts the cup in silence, or while saying:
The cup over which we give thanks is a sharing in the blood of Christ.

Giving the Bread and Cup

The bread and cup are given to the people, with these or other words being exchanged:
The body of Christ, given for you. **Amen.**
The blood of Christ, given for you. **Amen.**

Prayer after Receiving

Eternal God, we give you thanks for this holy mystery
    in which you have given yourself to us.
We live with joy
    in the knowledge that you make
        all good things possible.
Grant that we may go into the world
    in the strength of your Spirit,
        to give ourselves for others.
in the name of Jesus Christ our Lord.
Amen.

Proper 12 [July 24-30] (a)

Genesis 29:15-28; Psalm 105:1-11, 45b; Romans 8:26-39; Matthew 13:31-33, 44-52

The Lord be with you.
And also with you.
Lift up your hearts.
We lift them up to the Lord.
Let us give thanks to the Lord our God.
It is right to give our thanks and praise.

It is right, and a good and joyful thing
    always and everywhere to give thanks to you,
    Almighty God, Creator of heaven and earth.
Your Spirit helps us in our time of weakness.
Indeed, it intercedes for us
    with sighs too deep for words;
and nothing in life or in death can separate us
    from your great love.

And so, with your people on earth
    and all the company of heaven,
    we praise your name and join their unending hymn:

Holy, holy, holy Lord, God of power and might,
heaven and earth are full of your glory.
    Hosanna in the highest.
Blessed is he who comes in the name of the Lord.
    Hosanna in the highest.

Holy are you, and blessed is your Son Jesus Christ.
You did not withhold him from us,
    but gave him for us all.

Your Spirit anointed him
    to preach good news to the poor,
    to proclaim release to the captives and
    recovering of sight to the blind,
    to set at liberty those who are oppressed, and
    to announce that the time had come
    when you would save your people.
He healed the sick, fed the hungry, and ate with sinners.

By the baptism of his suffering, death, and resurrection,
   you gave birth to your church,
   delivered us from slavery to sin and death,
   and made with us a new covenant
   by water and the Spirit.

On the night in which he gave himself up for us
   he took bread, gave thanks to you, broke the bread,
   gave it to his disciples, and said,
"Take, eat; this is my body which is given for you.
Do this in remembrance of me."

When the supper was over he took the cup,
   gave thanks to you, gave it to his disciples, and said,
"Drink from this, all of you; this is my blood of the
   new covenant poured out for you and for many
      for the forgiveness of sins.
Do this as often as you drink it,
   in remembrance of me."

And so, in remembrance of these your mighty acts in Jesus Christ,
we offer ourselves in praise and thanksgiving
   as a holy and living sacrifice,
   in union with Christ's offering for us,
as we proclaim the mystery of faith.

Christ has died; Christ is risen; Christ will come again.

Pour out your Holy Spirit on us gathered here,
   and on these gifts of bread and wine.
Make them be for us the body and blood of Christ,
that we may be for the world the body of Christ,
   redeemed by his blood,
that we might be conformed
   in his image.

By your Spirit make us one with Christ,
   one with each other and
   one in ministry to all the world,
until Christ comes in final victory and
   we feast at the heavenly banquet.

Through your Son Jesus Christ,
with the Holy Spirit in your holy church,
all honor and glory is yours, almighty God,
    now and for ever.

Amen.

THE LORD'S PRAYER

And now with the confidence of children of God, let us pray: **Our Father...**

BREAKING THE BREAD

The pastor breaks the bread in silence, or while saying:
Because there is one loaf,
we, who are many, are one body, for we all partake of the one loaf.
The bread which we break is a sharing in the body of Christ.

The pastor lifts the cup in silence, or while saying:
The cup over which we give thanks is a sharing in the blood of Christ.

GIVING THE BREAD AND CUP

The bread and cup are given to the people, with these or other words being exchanged:
The body of Christ, given for you. **Amen.**
The blood of Christ, given for you. **Amen.**

PRAYER AFTER RECEIVING

Eternal God, we give you thanks for this holy mystery
    in which you have given yourself to us.
Let us be the yeast
    for the bread of life.
Grant that we may go into the world
    in the strength of your Spirit,
        to give ourselves for others.
in the name of Jesus Christ our Lord.
Amen.

Genesis 32:22-31; Psalm 17:1-7, 15; Romans 9:1-5; Matthew 14:13-21

The Lord be with you.
And also with you.
Lift up your hearts.
We lift them up to the Lord.
Let us give thanks to the Lord our God.
It is right to give our thanks and praise.

It is right, and a good and joyful thing
    always and everywhere to give thanks to you,
    Almighty God, Creator of heaven and earth.
You have given your people so many gifts;
    the glory, the covenants,
        the law, the worship, the promises.
But most important,
    you have given us your Messiah.

And so, with your people on earth
    and all the company of heaven,
    we praise your name and join their unending hymn:

Holy, holy, holy Lord, God of power and might,
heaven and earth are full of your glory.
    Hosanna in the highest.
Blessed is he who comes in the name of the Lord.
    Hosanna in the highest.

Holy are you, and blessed is your Son Jesus Christ.
He is the greatest gift you have given
    to the people you love.

Your Spirit anointed him
    to preach good news to the poor,
    to proclaim release to the captives and
    recovering of sight to the blind,
    to set at liberty those who are oppressed, and
    to announce that the time had come
    when you would save your people.
He healed the sick, fed the hungry, and ate with sinners.

By the baptism of his suffering, death, and resurrection,
    you gave birth to your church,
    delivered us from slavery to sin and death,
    and made with us a new covenant
    by water and the Spirit.

On the night in which he gave himself up for us
    he took bread, gave thanks to you, broke the bread,
    gave it to his disciples, and said,
"Take, eat; this is my body which is given for you.
Do this in remembrance of me."

When the supper was over he took the cup,
    gave thanks to you, gave it to his disciples, and said,
"Drink from this, all of you; this is my blood of the
    new covenant poured out for you and for many
        for the forgiveness of sins.
Do this as often as you drink it,
    in remembrance of me."

And so, in remembrance of these your mighty acts in Jesus Christ,
we offer ourselves in praise and thanksgiving
    as a holy and living sacrifice,
    in union with Christ's offering for us,
as we proclaim the mystery of faith.

Christ has died; Christ is risen; Christ will come again.

Pour out your Holy Spirit on us gathered here,
    and on these gifts of bread and wine.
Make them be for us the body and blood of Christ,
that we may be for the world the body of Christ,
    redeemed by his blood,
that we might share in all your holy gifts.

By your Spirit make us one with Christ,
    one with each other and
    one in ministry to all the world,
until Christ comes in final victory and
    we feast at the heavenly banquet.

Through your Son Jesus Christ,
with the Holy Spirit in your holy church,
all honor and glory is yours, almighty God,
    now and for ever.

Amen.

THE LORD'S PRAYER

And now with the confidence of children of God, let us pray: **Our Father...**

BREAKING THE BREAD

The pastor breaks the bread in silence, or while saying:
Because there is one loaf,
we, who are many, are one body, for we all partake of the one loaf.
The bread which we break is a sharing in the body of Christ.

The pastor lifts the cup in silence, or while saying:
The cup over which we give thanks is a sharing in the blood of Christ.

GIVING THE BREAD AND CUP

The bread and cup are given to the people, with these or other words being exchanged:
The body of Christ, given for you. **Amen.**
The blood of Christ, given for you. **Amen.**

PRAYER AFTER RECEIVING

Eternal God, we give you thanks for this holy mystery
    in which you have given yourself to us.
Your love empowers us
    to be a blessing to others.
Grant that we may go into the world
    in the strength of your Spirit,
    to give ourselves for others.
in the name of Jesus Christ our Lord.
Amen.

Genesis 37:1-4, 12-28; Psalm 105:1-6, 16-22, 45b; Romans 10:5-15; Matthew 14:22-33

The Lord be with you.
And also with you.
Lift up your hearts.
We lift them up to the Lord.
Let us give thanks to the Lord our God.
It is right to give our thanks and praise.

It is right, and a good and joyful thing
    always and everywhere to give thanks to you,
      Almighty God, Creator of heaven and earth.
You have made all people
    as your children;
all who call upon you in truth and faith
    shall be saved.

And so, with your people on earth
    and all the company of heaven,
    we praise your name and join their unending hymn:

Holy, holy, holy Lord, God of power and might,
heaven and earth are full of your glory.
    Hosanna in the highest.
Blessed is he who comes in the name of the Lord.
    Hosanna in the highest.

Holy are you, and blessed is your Son Jesus Christ.
He came to lead all the world
    into your loving arms.

Your Spirit anointed him
    to preach good news to the poor,
    to proclaim release to the captives and
    recovering of sight to the blind,
    to set at liberty those who are oppressed, and
    to announce that the time had come
    when you would save your people.
He healed the sick, fed the hungry, and ate with sinners.

By the baptism of his suffering, death, and resurrection,
    you gave birth to your church,
    delivered us from slavery to sin and death,
    and made with us a new covenant
    by water and the Spirit.

On the night in which he gave himself up for us
    he took bread, gave thanks to you, broke the bread,
    gave it to his disciples, and said,
"Take, eat; this is my body which is given for you.
Do this in remembrance of me."

When the supper was over he took the cup,
    gave thanks to you, gave it to his disciples, and said,
"Drink from this, all of you; this is my blood of the
    new covenant poured out for you and for many
        for the forgiveness of sins.
Do this as often as you drink it,
    in remembrance of me."

And so, in remembrance of these your mighty acts in Jesus Christ,
we offer ourselves in praise and thanksgiving
    as a holy and living sacrifice,
    in union with Christ's offering for us,
as we proclaim the mystery of faith.

Christ has died; Christ is risen; Christ will come again.

Pour out your Holy Spirit on us gathered here,
    and on these gifts of bread and wine.
Make them be for us the body and blood of Christ,
that we may be for the world the body of Christ,
    redeemed by his blood,
for no one who believes in him
    will be put to shame.

By your Spirit make us one with Christ,
    one with each other and
    one in ministry to all the world,
until Christ comes in final victory and
    we feast at the heavenly banquet.

Through your Son Jesus Christ,
with the Holy Spirit in your holy church,
all honor and glory is yours, almighty God,
    now and for ever.

Amen.

THE LORD'S PRAYER

And now with the confidence of children of God, let us pray: **Our Father...**

BREAKING THE BREAD

The pastor breaks the bread in silence, or while saying:
Because there is one loaf,
we, who are many, are one body, for we all partake of the one loaf.
The bread which we break is a sharing in the body of Christ.

The pastor lifts the cup in silence, or while saying:
The cup over which we give thanks is a sharing in the blood of Christ.

GIVING THE BREAD AND CUP

The bread and cup are given to the people, with these or other words being exchanged:
The body of Christ, given for you. **Amen.**
The blood of Christ, given for you. **Amen.**

PRAYER AFTER RECEIVING

Eternal God, we give you thanks for this holy mystery
    in which you have given yourself to us.
Help us live out in our lives
    what we believe in our hearts.
And may what we believe in our hearts
    be proclaimed with our mouths.
Grant that we may go into the world
    in the strength of your Spirit,
    to give ourselves for others.
in the name of Jesus Christ our Lord.
Amen.

Genesis 45:1-15; Psalm 133; Romans 11:1-2a, 29-32; Matthew 15:(10-20) 21-28

The Lord be with you.
And also with you.
Lift up your hearts.
We lift them up to the Lord.
Let us give thanks to the Lord our God.
It is right to give our thanks and praise.

It is right, and a good and joyful thing
    always and everywhere to give thanks to you,
    Almighty God, Creator of heaven and earth.
How merciful you are, O Lord.
Even when your people disobey,
    you redeem them
        as you did Joseph's family.

And so, with your people on earth
    and all the company of heaven,
    we praise your name and join their unending hymn:

Holy, holy, holy Lord, God of power and might,
heaven and earth are full of your glory.
    Hosanna in the highest.
Blessed is he who comes in the name of the Lord.
    Hosanna in the highest.

Holy are you, and blessed is your Son Jesus Christ.
He has opened your love
    to all the world.

Your Spirit anointed him
    to preach good news to the poor,
    to proclaim release to the captives and
    recovering of sight to the blind,
    to set at liberty those who are oppressed, and
    to announce that the time had come
    when you would save your people.
He healed the sick, fed the hungry, and ate with sinners.

By the baptism of his suffering, death, and resurrection,
    you gave birth to your church,
    delivered us from slavery to sin and death,
    and made with us a new covenant
    by water and the Spirit.

On the night in which he gave himself up for us
    he took bread, gave thanks to you, broke the bread,
    gave it to his disciples, and said,
"Take, eat; this is my body which is given for you.
Do this in remembrance of me."

When the supper was over he took the cup,
    gave thanks to you, gave it to his disciples, and said,
"Drink from this, all of you; this is my blood of the
    new covenant poured out for you and for many
        for the forgiveness of sins.
Do this as often as you drink it,
    in remembrance of me."

And so, in remembrance of these your mighty acts in Jesus Christ,
we offer ourselves in praise and thanksgiving
    as a holy and living sacrifice,
    in union with Christ's offering for us,
as we proclaim the mystery of faith.

Christ has died; Christ is risen; Christ will come again.

Pour out your Holy Spirit on us gathered here,
    and on these gifts of bread and wine.
Make them be for us the body and blood of Christ,
that we may be for the world the body of Christ,
    redeemed by his blood,
that we might know and share
    your love for all humanity.

By your Spirit make us one with Christ,
    one with each other and
    one in ministry to all the world,
until Christ comes in final victory and
    we feast at the heavenly banquet.

 O'Donnell, *Lift Up Your Hearts 3rd ed. Year A*

Through your Son Jesus Christ,
with the Holy Spirit in your holy church,
all honor and glory is yours, almighty God,
    now and for ever.

Amen.

THE LORD'S PRAYER

And now with the confidence of children of God, let us pray: **Our Father...**

BREAKING THE BREAD

The pastor breaks the bread in silence, or while saying:
Because there is one loaf,
we, who are many, are one body, for we all partake of the one loaf.
The bread which we break is a sharing in the body of Christ.

The pastor lifts the cup in silence, or while saying:
The cup over which we give thanks is a sharing in the blood of Christ.

GIVING THE BREAD AND CUP

The bread and cup are given to the people, with these or other words being exchanged:
The body of Christ, given for you. **Amen.**
The blood of Christ, given for you. **Amen.**

PRAYER AFTER RECEIVING

Eternal God, we give you thanks for this holy mystery
    in which you have given yourself to us.
May we never judge
    who can or cannot receive
        the benefits of your love.
Grant that we may go into the world
    in the strength of your Spirit,
        to give ourselves for others.
in the name of Jesus Christ our Lord.
Amen.

Proper 16 [August 21-27] (a)

Exodus 1:8-2:10; Psalm 124; Romans 12:1-8; Matthew 16:13-20

The Lord be with you.
And also with you.
Lift up your hearts.
We lift them up to the Lord.
Let us give thanks to the Lord our God.
It is right to give our thanks and praise.

It is right, and a good and joyful thing
    always and everywhere to give thanks to you,
    Almighty God, Creator of heaven and earth.
When Pharaoh ordered all Hebrew boys
    to be murdered at birth,
you saved Moses by water
    and placed him
        in Pharaoh's own house.

And so, with your people on earth
    and all the company of heaven,
    we praise your name and join their unending hymn:

Holy, holy, holy Lord, God of power and might,
heaven and earth are full of your glory.
    Hosanna in the highest.
Blessed is he who comes in the name of the Lord.
    Hosanna in the highest.

Holy are you, and blessed is your Son Jesus Christ.
You revealed him to Peter
    as the Messiah.

Your Spirit anointed him
    to preach good news to the poor,
    to proclaim release to the captives and
    recovering of sight to the blind,
    to set at liberty those who are oppressed, and
    to announce that the time had come
    when you would save your people.
He healed the sick, fed the hungry, and ate with sinners.

By the baptism of his suffering, death, and resurrection,
 you gave birth to your church,
 delivered us from slavery to sin and death,
 and made with us a new covenant
 by water and the Spirit.

On the night in which he gave himself up for us
 he took bread, gave thanks to you, broke the bread,
 gave it to his disciples, and said,
"Take, eat; this is my body which is given for you.
Do this in remembrance of me."

When the supper was over he took the cup,
 gave thanks to you, gave it to his disciples, and said,
"Drink from this, all of you; this is my blood of the
 new covenant poured out for you and for many
  for the forgiveness of sins.
Do this as often as you drink it,
 in remembrance of me."

And so, in remembrance of these your mighty acts in Jesus Christ,
we offer ourselves in praise and thanksgiving
 as a holy and living sacrifice,
 in union with Christ's offering for us,
as we proclaim the mystery of faith.

Christ has died; Christ is risen; Christ will come again.

Pour out your Holy Spirit on us gathered here,
 and on these gifts of bread and wine.
Make them be for us the body and blood of Christ,
that we may be for the world the body of Christ,
 redeemed by his blood,
that we may be living sacrifices,
 holy and acceptable to you.

By your Spirit make us one with Christ,
 one with each other and
 one in ministry to all the world,
until Christ comes in final victory and
 we feast at the heavenly banquet.

Through your Son Jesus Christ,
with the Holy Spirit in your holy church,
all honor and glory is yours, almighty God,
    now and for ever.

Amen.

THE LORD'S PRAYER

And now with the confidence of children of God, let us pray: **Our Father...**

BREAKING THE BREAD

The pastor breaks the bread in silence, or while saying:
Because there is one loaf,
we, who are many, are one body, for we all partake of the one loaf.
The bread which we break is a sharing in the body of Christ.

The pastor lifts the cup in silence, or while saying:
The cup over which we give thanks is a sharing in the blood of Christ.

GIVING THE BREAD AND CUP

The bread and cup are given to the people, with these or other words being exchanged:
The body of Christ, given for you. **Amen.**
The blood of Christ, given for you. **Amen.**

PRAYER AFTER RECEIVING

Eternal God, we give you thanks for this holy mystery
    in which you have given yourself to us.
May we each do as called
    according to the grace given us.
Grant that we may go into the world
    in the strength of your Spirit,
        to give ourselves for others.
in the name of Jesus Christ our Lord.
Amen.

The Lord be with you.
And also with you.
Lift up your hearts.
We lift them up to the Lord.
Let us give thanks to the Lord our God.
It is right to give our thanks and praise.

It is right, and a good and joyful thing
    always and everywhere to give thanks to you,
    Almighty God, Creator of heaven and earth.
You heard the cry of your people in slavery.
You hear our cries, as well
    and deliver us through our pain.

And so, with your people on earth
    and all the company of heaven,
    we praise your name and join their unending hymn:

Holy, holy, holy Lord, God of power and might,
heaven and earth are full of your glory.
    Hosanna in the highest.
Blessed is he who comes in the name of the Lord.
    Hosanna in the highest.

Holy are you, and blessed is your Son Jesus Christ.
He knew he was called
    to suffer and die
        for the sins of the world;
and yet he did not shy from it.

Your Spirit anointed him
    to preach good news to the poor,
    to proclaim release to the captives and
    recovering of sight to the blind,
    to set at liberty those who are oppressed, and
    to announce that the time had come
    when you would save your people.
He healed the sick, fed the hungry, and ate with sinners.

By the baptism of his suffering, death, and resurrection,
    you gave birth to your church,
    delivered us from slavery to sin and death,
    and made with us a new covenant
    by water and the Spirit.

On the night in which he gave himself up for us
    he took bread, gave thanks to you, broke the bread,
    gave it to his disciples, and said,
"Take, eat; this is my body which is given for you.
Do this in remembrance of me."

When the supper was over he took the cup,
    gave thanks to you, gave it to his disciples, and said,
"Drink from this, all of you; this is my blood of the
    new covenant poured out for you and for many
        for the forgiveness of sins.
Do this as often as you drink it,
    in remembrance of me."

And so, in remembrance of these your mighty acts in Jesus Christ,
we offer ourselves in praise and thanksgiving
    as a holy and living sacrifice,
    in union with Christ's offering for us,
as we proclaim the mystery of faith.

Christ has died; Christ is risen; Christ will come again.

Pour out your Holy Spirit on us gathered here,
    and on these gifts of bread and wine.
Make them be for us the body and blood of Christ,
that we may be for the world the body of Christ,
    redeemed by his blood,
that all people might rejoice
    in hope.

By your Spirit make us one with Christ,
    one with each other and
    one in ministry to all the world,
until Christ comes in final victory and
    we feast at the heavenly banquet.

Through your Son Jesus Christ,
with the Holy Spirit in your holy church,
all honor and glory is yours, almighty God,
    now and for ever.

Amen.

THE LORD'S PRAYER
And now with the confidence of children of God, let us pray: **Our Father...**

BREAKING THE BREAD
The pastor breaks the bread in silence, or while saying:
Because there is one loaf,
we, who are many, are one body, for we all partake of the one loaf.
The bread which we break is a sharing in the body of Christ.

The pastor lifts the cup in silence, or while saying:
The cup over which we give thanks is a sharing in the blood of Christ.

GIVING THE BREAD AND CUP
The bread and cup are given to the people, with these or other words being exchanged:
The body of Christ, given for you. **Amen.**
The blood of Christ, given for you. **Amen.**

PRAYER AFTER RECEIVING
Eternal God, we give you thanks for this holy mystery
    in which you have given yourself to us.
Let us rejoice in hope,
    be patient in suffering,
        and have perseverance in prayer.
Grant that we may go into the world
    in the strength of your Spirit,
    to give ourselves for others.
in the name of Jesus Christ our Lord.
Amen.

Proper 18 [September 4-10] (a)

Exodus 12:1-14; Psalm 149 or Psalm 148; Romans 13:8-14; Matthew 18:15-20

The Lord be with you.
And also with you.
Lift up your hearts.
We lift them up to the Lord.
Let us give thanks to the Lord our God.
It is right to give our thanks and praise.

It is right, and a good and joyful thing
    always and everywhere to give thanks to you,
    Almighty God, Creator of heaven and earth.
You gave your people
    the sign of blood
        to save them from the angel of death.

And so, with your people on earth
    and all the company of heaven,
    we praise your name and join their unending hymn:

Holy, holy, holy Lord, God of power and might,
heaven and earth are full of your glory.
    Hosanna in the highest.
Blessed is he who comes in the name of the Lord.
    Hosanna in the highest.

Holy are you, and blessed is your Son Jesus Christ.
He is our Passover Lamb;
    all who accept his sacrifice
        for their sins
    gain eternal life.

Your Spirit anointed him
    to preach good news to the poor,
    to proclaim release to the captives and
    recovering of sight to the blind,
    to set at liberty those who are oppressed, and
    to announce that the time had come
    when you would save your people.
He healed the sick, fed the hungry, and ate with sinners.

By the baptism of his suffering, death, and resurrection,
    you gave birth to your church,
    delivered us from slavery to sin and death,
    and made with us a new covenant
    by water and the Spirit.

On the night in which he gave himself up for us
    he took bread, gave thanks to you, broke the bread,
    gave it to his disciples, and said,
"Take, eat; this is my body which is given for you.
Do this in remembrance of me."

When the supper was over he took the cup,
    gave thanks to you, gave it to his disciples, and said,
"Drink from this, all of you; this is my blood of the
    new covenant poured out for you and for many
        for the forgiveness of sins.
Do this as often as you drink it,
    in remembrance of me."

And so, in remembrance of these your mighty acts in Jesus Christ,
we offer ourselves in praise and thanksgiving
    as a holy and living sacrifice,
    in union with Christ's offering for us,
as we proclaim the mystery of faith.

Christ has died; Christ is risen; Christ will come again.

Pour out your Holy Spirit on us gathered here,
    and on these gifts of bread and wine.
Make them be for us the body and blood of Christ,
that we may be for the world the body of Christ,
    redeemed by his blood,
that all the world
    might live in love.

By your Spirit make us one with Christ,
    one with each other and
    one in ministry to all the world,
until Christ comes in final victory and
    we feast at the heavenly banquet.

Through your Son Jesus Christ,
with the Holy Spirit in your holy church,
all honor and glory is yours, almighty God,
    now and for ever.

Amen.

THE LORD'S PRAYER
And now with the confidence of children of God, let us pray: **Our Father...**

BREAKING THE BREAD
The pastor breaks the bread in silence, or while saying:
Because there is one loaf,
we, who are many, are one body, for we all partake of the one loaf.
The bread which we break is a sharing in the body of Christ.

The pastor lifts the cup in silence, or while saying:
The cup over which we give thanks is a sharing in the blood of Christ.

GIVING THE BREAD AND CUP
The bread and cup are given to the people, with these or other words being exchanged:
The body of Christ, given for you. **Amen.**
The blood of Christ, given for you. **Amen.**

PRAYER AFTER RECEIVING
Eternal God, we give you thanks for this holy mystery
    in which you have given yourself to us.
Let our every act and word and deed
    be an act of love.
Grant that we may go into the world
    in the strength of your Spirit,
    to give ourselves for others.
in the name of Jesus Christ our Lord.
Amen.

Proper 19 [September 11-17] (a)

Exodus 14:19-31; Exodus 15:1b-11, 20-21 or Psalm 114; Romans 14:1-12; Matthew 18:21-35

The Lord be with you.
And also with you.
Lift up your hearts.
We lift them up to the Lord.
Let us give thanks to the Lord our God.
It is right to give our thanks and praise.

It is right, and a good and joyful thing
    always and everywhere to give thanks to you,
    Almighty God, Creator of heaven and earth.
Who is like you, O Lord?
Who is like you, majestic in holiness,
    awesome in splendor, doing wondrous things?
Let us sing to you, O Lord Most High.

And so, with your people on earth
    and all the company of heaven,
    we praise your name and join their unending hymn:

Holy, holy, holy Lord, God of power and might,
heaven and earth are full of your glory.
    Hosanna in the highest.
Blessed is he who comes in the name of the Lord.
    Hosanna in the highest.

Holy are you, and blessed is your Son Jesus Christ.
He taught us that your way
    is always to show forgiveness
        and mercy.

Your Spirit anointed him
    to preach good news to the poor,
    to proclaim release to the captives and
    recovering of sight to the blind,
    to set at liberty those who are oppressed, and
    to announce that the time had come
    when you would save your people.
He healed the sick, fed the hungry, and ate with sinners.

By the baptism of his suffering, death, and resurrection,
    you gave birth to your church,
    delivered us from slavery to sin and death,
    and made with us a new covenant
    by water and the Spirit.

On the night in which he gave himself up for us
    he took bread, gave thanks to you, broke the bread,
    gave it to his disciples, and said,
"Take, eat; this is my body which is given for you.
Do this in remembrance of me."

When the supper was over he took the cup,
    gave thanks to you, gave it to his disciples, and said,
"Drink from this, all of you; this is my blood of the
    new covenant poured out for you and for many
        for the forgiveness of sins.
Do this as often as you drink it,
    in remembrance of me."

And so, in remembrance of these your mighty acts in Jesus Christ,
we offer ourselves in praise and thanksgiving
    as a holy and living sacrifice,
    in union with Christ's offering for us,
as we proclaim the mystery of faith.

Christ has died; Christ is risen; Christ will come again.

Pour out your Holy Spirit on us gathered here,
    and on these gifts of bread and wine.
Make them be for us the body and blood of Christ,
that we may be for the world the body of Christ,
    redeemed by his blood,
for he is Lord
    of the living and the dead.

By your Spirit make us one with Christ,
    one with each other and
    one in ministry to all the world,
until Christ comes in final victory and
    we feast at the heavenly banquet.

O'Donnell, Lift Up Your Hearts 3rd ed. Year A

Through your Son Jesus Christ,
with the Holy Spirit in your holy church,
all honor and glory is yours, almighty God,
    now and for ever.

Amen.

The Lord's Prayer

And now with the confidence of children of God, let us pray: **Our Father...**

Breaking the Bread

The pastor breaks the bread in silence, or while saying:
Because there is one loaf,
we, who are many, are one body, for we all partake of the one loaf.
The bread which we break is a sharing in the body of Christ.

The pastor lifts the cup in silence, or while saying:
The cup over which we give thanks is a sharing in the blood of Christ.

Giving the Bread and Cup

The bread and cup are given to the people, with these or other words being exchanged:
The body of Christ, given for you. **Amen.**
The blood of Christ, given for you. **Amen.**

Prayer after Receiving

Eternal God, we give you thanks for this holy mystery
    in which you have given yourself to us.
Empower us to live
    not to ourselves,
        but to you.
And when we die,
    may we die to you.
Grant that we may go into the world
    in the strength of your Spirit,
    to give ourselves for others.
in the name of Jesus Christ our Lord.
Amen.

Exodus 16:2-15; Psalm 105:1-6, 37-45 or Psalm 78; Philippians 1:21-30; Matthew 20:1-16

The Lord be with you.
And also with you.
Lift up your hearts.
We lift them up to the Lord.
Let us give thanks to the Lord our God.
It is right to give our thanks and praise.

It is right, and a good and joyful thing
    always and everywhere to give thanks to you,
    Almighty God, Creator of heaven and earth.
You freed your people from slavery
    but still they complained against you.
In response
    you gave them manna from heaven.

And so, with your people on earth
    and all the company of heaven,
    we praise your name and join their unending hymn:

Holy, holy, holy Lord, God of power and might,
heaven and earth are full of your glory.
    Hosanna in the highest.
Blessed is he who comes in the name of the Lord.
    Hosanna in the highest.

Holy are you, and blessed is your Son Jesus Christ.
He taught us that
    your ways are not our ways;
    your laws are not our laws

Your Spirit anointed him
    to preach good news to the poor,
    to proclaim release to the captives and
    recovering of sight to the blind,
    to set at liberty those who are oppressed, and
    to announce that the time had come
    when you would save your people.
He healed the sick, fed the hungry, and ate with sinners.

By the baptism of his suffering, death, and resurrection,
    you gave birth to your church,
    delivered us from slavery to sin and death,
    and made with us a new covenant
    by water and the Spirit.

On the night in which he gave himself up for us
    he took bread, gave thanks to you, broke the bread,
    gave it to his disciples, and said,
"Take, eat; this is my body which is given for you.
Do this in remembrance of me."

When the supper was over he took the cup,
    gave thanks to you, gave it to his disciples, and said,
"Drink from this, all of you; this is my blood of the
    new covenant poured out for you and for many
        for the forgiveness of sins.
Do this as often as you drink it,
    in remembrance of me."

And so, in remembrance of these your mighty acts in Jesus Christ,
we offer ourselves in praise and thanksgiving
    as a holy and living sacrifice,
    in union with Christ's offering for us,
as we proclaim the mystery of faith.

Christ has died; Christ is risen; Christ will come again.

Pour out your Holy Spirit on us gathered here,
    and on these gifts of bread and wine.
Make them be for us the body and blood of Christ,
that we may be for the world the body of Christ,
    redeemed by his blood,
that we might be a means of justice and love
    in the world.

By your Spirit make us one with Christ,
    one with each other and
    one in ministry to all the world,
until Christ comes in final victory and
    we feast at the heavenly banquet.

Through your Son Jesus Christ,
with the Holy Spirit in your holy church,
all honor and glory is yours, almighty God,
    now and for ever.

Amen.

THE LORD'S PRAYER

And now with the confidence of children of God, let us pray: **Our Father...**

BREAKING THE BREAD

The pastor breaks the bread in silence, or while saying:
Because there is one loaf,
we, who are many, are one body, for we all partake of the one loaf.
The bread which we break is a sharing in the body of Christ.

The pastor lifts the cup in silence, or while saying:
The cup over which we give thanks is a sharing in the blood of Christ.

GIVING THE BREAD AND CUP

The bread and cup are given to the people, with these or other words being exchanged:
The body of Christ, given for you. **Amen.**
The blood of Christ, given for you. **Amen.**

PRAYER AFTER RECEIVING

Eternal God, we give you thanks for this holy mystery
    in which you have given yourself to us.
May our lives reflect
    your generosity, mercy and love
        in all our actions.
Grant that we may go into the world
    in the strength of your Spirit,
        to give ourselves for others.
in the name of Jesus Christ our Lord.
Amen.

Exodus 17:1-7; Psalm 78:1-4, 12-16; Philippians 2:1-13; Matthew 21:23-32

The Lord be with you.
And also with you.
Lift up your hearts.
We lift them up to the Lord.
Let us give thanks to the Lord our God.
It is right to give our thanks and praise.

It is right, and a good and joyful thing
    always and everywhere to give thanks to you,
    Almighty God, Creator of heaven and earth.
You led your people through the wilderness
    and when they grew thirsty and complained against you
       you gave them water from the rock.

And so, with your people on earth
    and all the company of heaven,
    we praise your name and join their unending hymn:

Holy, holy, holy Lord, God of power and might,
heaven and earth are full of your glory.
    Hosanna in the highest.
Blessed is he who comes in the name of the Lord.
    Hosanna in the highest.

Holy are you, and blessed is your Son Jesus Christ.
He did not regard equality with you as something to be exploited,
but emptied himself, taking the form of a slave,
    being born in human likeness.
He humbled himself and became obedient
    to the point of death—even death on a cross

Your Spirit anointed him
    to preach good news to the poor,
    to proclaim release to the captives and
    recovering of sight to the blind,
    to set at liberty those who are oppressed, and
    to announce that the time had come
    when you would save your people.

He healed the sick, fed the hungry, and ate with sinners.
By the baptism of his suffering, death, and resurrection,
    you gave birth to your church,
    delivered us from slavery to sin and death,
    and made with us a new covenant
    by water and the Spirit.

On the night in which he gave himself up for us
    he took bread, gave thanks to you, broke the bread,
    gave it to his disciples, and said,
"Take, eat; this is my body which is given for you.
Do this in remembrance of me."

When the supper was over he took the cup,
    gave thanks to you, gave it to his disciples, and said,
"Drink from this, all of you; this is my blood of the
    new covenant poured out for you and for many
        for the forgiveness of sins.
Do this as often as you drink it,
    in remembrance of me."

And so, in remembrance of these your mighty acts in Jesus Christ,
we offer ourselves in praise and thanksgiving
    as a holy and living sacrifice,
    in union with Christ's offering for us,
as we proclaim the mystery of faith.

Christ has died; Christ is risen; Christ will come again.

Pour out your Holy Spirit on us gathered here,
    and on these gifts of bread and wine.
Make them be for us the body and blood of Christ,
that we may be for the world the body of Christ,
    redeemed by his blood,
that we may have the same mind as Christ.

By your Spirit make us one with Christ,
    one with each other and
    one in ministry to all the world,
until Christ comes in final victory and
    we feast at the heavenly banquet.

Through your Son Jesus Christ,
with the Holy Spirit in your holy church,
all honor and glory is yours, almighty God,
    now and for ever.

Amen.

THE LORD'S PRAYER
And now with the confidence of children of God, let us pray: **Our Father...**

BREAKING THE BREAD
The pastor breaks the bread in silence, or while saying:
Because there is one loaf,
we, who are many, are one body, for we all partake of the one loaf.
The bread which we break is a sharing in the body of Christ.

The pastor lifts the cup in silence, or while saying:
The cup over which we give thanks is a sharing in the blood of Christ.

GIVING THE BREAD AND CUP
The bread and cup are given to the people, with these or other words being exchanged:
The body of Christ, given for you. **Amen.**
The blood of Christ, given for you. **Amen.**

PRAYER AFTER RECEIVING
Eternal God, we give you thanks for this holy mystery
    in which you have given yourself to us.
Let our hearts and mouths declare
    Jesus Christ is Lord.
Grant that we may go into the world
    in the strength of your Spirit,
    to give ourselves for others.
in the name of Jesus Christ our Lord.
Amen.

Exodus 20:1-4, 7-9, 12-20; Psalm 19; Philippians 3:4b-14; Matthew 21:33-46

The Lord be with you.
And also with you.
Lift up your hearts.
We lift them up to the Lord.
Let us give thanks to the Lord our God.
It is right to give our thanks and praise.

It is right, and a good and joyful thing
    always and everywhere to give thanks to you,
    Almighty God, Creator of heaven and earth.
The heavens are telling your glory, O Lord;
    and the firmament proclaims your handiwork.
Your law is perfect; it revives the soul.
Your decrees are sure, making wise the simple.

And so, with your people on earth
    and all the company of heaven,
    we praise your name and join their unending hymn:

Holy, holy, holy Lord, God of power and might,
heaven and earth are full of your glory.
    Hosanna in the highest.
Blessed is he who comes in the name of the Lord.
    Hosanna in the highest.

Holy are you, and blessed is your Son Jesus Christ.
He has fulfilled the law, freeing us for obedience in faith.
But he has rejected those who used the Law
    for their own personal gain.

Your Spirit anointed him
    to preach good news to the poor,
    to proclaim release to the captives and
    recovering of sight to the blind,
    to set at liberty those who are oppressed, and
    to announce that the time had come
    when you would save your people.
He healed the sick, fed the hungry, and ate with sinners.

By the baptism of his suffering, death, and resurrection,
    you gave birth to your church,
    delivered us from slavery to sin and death,
    and made with us a new covenant
    by water and the Spirit.

On the night in which he gave himself up for us
    he took bread, gave thanks to you, broke the bread,
    gave it to his disciples, and said,
"Take, eat; this is my body which is given for you.
Do this in remembrance of me."

When the supper was over he took the cup,
    gave thanks to you, gave it to his disciples, and said,
"Drink from this, all of you; this is my blood of the
    new covenant poured out for you and for many
        for the forgiveness of sins.
Do this as often as you drink it,
    in remembrance of me."

And so, in remembrance of these your mighty acts in Jesus Christ,
we offer ourselves in praise and thanksgiving
    as a holy and living sacrifice,
    in union with Christ's offering for us,
as we proclaim the mystery of faith.

Christ has died; Christ is risen; Christ will come again.

Pour out your Holy Spirit on us gathered here,
    and on these gifts of bread and wine.
Make them be for us the body and blood of Christ,
that we may be for the world the body of Christ,
    redeemed by his blood,
as we press toward the goal for the prize
    of your heavenly call.

By your Spirit make us one with Christ,
    one with each other and
    one in ministry to all the world,
until Christ comes in final victory and
    we feast at the heavenly banquet.

Through your Son Jesus Christ,
with the Holy Spirit in your holy church,
all honor and glory is yours, almighty God,
    now and for ever.

Amen.

THE LORD'S PRAYER
And now with the confidence of children of God, let us pray: **Our Father...**

BREAKING THE BREAD
The pastor breaks the bread in silence, or while saying:
Because there is one loaf,
we, who are many, are one body, for we all partake of the one loaf.
The bread which we break is a sharing in the body of Christ.

The pastor lifts the cup in silence, or while saying:
The cup over which we give thanks is a sharing in the blood of Christ.

GIVING THE BREAD AND CUP
The bread and cup are given to the people, with these or other words being exchanged:
The body of Christ, given for you. **Amen.**
The blood of Christ, given for you. **Amen.**

PRAYER AFTER RECEIVING
Eternal God, we give you thanks for this holy mystery
    in which you have given yourself to us.
Help us to measure our gains
    not in earthly terms,
        but in faith.
Grant that we may go into the world
    in the strength of your Spirit,
    to give ourselves for others.
in the name of Jesus Christ our Lord.
Amen.

Exodus 32:1-14; Psalm 106:1-6, 19-23; Philippians 4:1-9; Matthew 22:1-14

The Lord be with you.
And also with you.
Lift up your hearts.
We lift them up to the Lord.
Let us give thanks to the Lord our God.
It is right to give our thanks and praise.

It is right, and a good and joyful thing
    always and everywhere to give thanks to you,
    Almighty God, Creator of heaven and earth.
When the people turned against you,
    built a golden calf and called it their god,
        your wrath burned hot against them.
But Moses reminded you of your promise to Abraham;
    you relented and let them live.

And so, with your people on earth
    and all the company of heaven,
    we praise your name and join their unending hymn:

Holy, holy, holy Lord, God of power and might,
heaven and earth are full of your glory.
    Hosanna in the highest.
Blessed is he who comes in the name of the Lord.
    Hosanna in the highest.

Holy are you, and blessed is your Son Jesus Christ.
He invites all to feast in your love,
    but many reject him.

Your Spirit anointed him
    to preach good news to the poor,
    to proclaim release to the captives and
    recovering of sight to the blind,
    to set at liberty those who are oppressed, and
    to announce that the time had come
    when you would save your people.
He healed the sick, fed the hungry, and ate with sinners.

By the baptism of his suffering, death, and resurrection,
    you gave birth to your church,
    delivered us from slavery to sin and death,
    and made with us a new covenant
    by water and the Spirit.

On the night in which he gave himself up for us
    he took bread, gave thanks to you, broke the bread,
    gave it to his disciples, and said,
"Take, eat; this is my body which is given for you.
Do this in remembrance of me."

When the supper was over he took the cup,
    gave thanks to you, gave it to his disciples, and said,
"Drink from this, all of you; this is my blood of the
    new covenant poured out for you and for many
        for the forgiveness of sins.
Do this as often as you drink it,
    in remembrance of me."

And so, in remembrance of these your mighty acts in Jesus Christ,
we offer ourselves in praise and thanksgiving
    as a holy and living sacrifice,
    in union with Christ's offering for us,
as we proclaim the mystery of faith.

Christ has died; Christ is risen; Christ will come again.

Pour out your Holy Spirit on us gathered here,
    and on these gifts of bread and wine.
Make them be for us the body and blood of Christ,
that we may be for the world the body of Christ,
    redeemed by his blood,
that through it all people might know
    that they are invited to your feast.

By your Spirit make us one with Christ,
    one with each other and
    one in ministry to all the world,
until Christ comes in final victory and
    we feast at the heavenly banquet.

Through your Son Jesus Christ,
with the Holy Spirit in your holy church,
all honor and glory is yours, almighty God,
     now and for ever.

Amen.

THE LORD'S PRAYER

And now with the confidence of children of God, let us pray: **Our Father...**

BREAKING THE BREAD

The pastor breaks the bread in silence, or while saying:
Because there is one loaf,
we, who are many, are one body, for we all partake of the one loaf.
The bread which we break is a sharing in the body of Christ.

The pastor lifts the cup in silence, or while saying:
The cup over which we give thanks is a sharing in the blood of Christ.

GIVING THE BREAD AND CUP

The bread and cup are given to the people, with these or other words being exchanged:
The body of Christ, given for you. **Amen.**
The blood of Christ, given for you. **Amen.**

PRAYER AFTER RECEIVING

Eternal God, we give you thanks for this holy mystery
     in which you have given yourself to us.
Let us worry about nothing,
     but come to you in prayer and supplication
          with thanksgiving.
Grant that we may go into the world
     in the strength of your Spirit,
          to give ourselves for others.
in the name of Jesus Christ our Lord.
Amen.

*NOTE: A benediction from Philippians 4:4-7 or Philippians 4:8-9 (see page 221)
     would be especially appropriate this Sunday.*

Exodus 33:12-23; Psalm 99; 1 Thessalonians 1:1-10; Matthew 22:15-22

The Lord be with you.
And also with you.
Lift up your hearts.
We lift them up to the Lord.
Let us give thanks to the Lord our God.
It is right to give our thanks and praise.

It is right, and a good and joyful thing
    always and everywhere to give thanks to you,
    Almighty God, Creator of heaven and earth.
You are the Mighty King,
    lover of justice;
you have established equity;
you have executed justice and righteousness.

And so, with your people on earth
    and all the company of heaven,
    we praise your name and join their unending hymn:

Holy, holy, holy Lord, God of power and might,
heaven and earth are full of your glory.
    Hosanna in the highest.
Blessed is he who comes in the name of the Lord.
    Hosanna in the highest.

Holy are you, and blessed is your Son Jesus Christ.
He showed not partiality.
He treated all with respect
    as he showed them the path to you.

Your Spirit anointed him
    to preach good news to the poor,
    to proclaim release to the captives and
    recovering of sight to the blind,
    to set at liberty those who are oppressed, and
    to announce that the time had come
    when you would save your people.
He healed the sick, fed the hungry, and ate with sinners.

By the baptism of his suffering, death, and resurrection,
    you gave birth to your church,
    delivered us from slavery to sin and death,
    and made with us a new covenant
    by water and the Spirit.

On the night in which he gave himself up for us
    he took bread, gave thanks to you, broke the bread,
    gave it to his disciples, and said,
"Take, eat; this is my body which is given for you.
Do this in remembrance of me."

When the supper was over he took the cup,
    gave thanks to you, gave it to his disciples, and said,
"Drink from this, all of you; this is my blood of the
    new covenant poured out for you and for many
        for the forgiveness of sins.
Do this as often as you drink it,
    in remembrance of me."

And so, in remembrance of these your mighty acts in Jesus Christ,
we offer ourselves in praise and thanksgiving
    as a holy and living sacrifice,
    in union with Christ's offering for us,
as we proclaim the mystery of faith.

Christ has died; Christ is risen; Christ will come again.

Pour out your Holy Spirit on us gathered here,
    and on these gifts of bread and wine.
Make them be for us the body and blood of Christ,
that we may be for the world the body of Christ,
    redeemed by his blood,
that we might be imitators of Christ
    in all things.

By your Spirit make us one with Christ,
    one with each other and
    one in ministry to all the world,
until Christ comes in final victory and
    we feast at the heavenly banquet.

Through your Son Jesus Christ,
with the Holy Spirit in your holy church,
all honor and glory is yours, almighty God,
     now and for ever.

Amen.

THE LORD'S PRAYER
And now with the confidence of children of God, let us pray: **Our Father...**

BREAKING THE BREAD
The pastor breaks the bread in silence, or while saying:
Because there is one loaf,
we, who are many, are one body, for we all partake of the one loaf.
The bread which we break is a sharing in the body of Christ.

The pastor lifts the cup in silence, or while saying:
The cup over which we give thanks is a sharing in the blood of Christ.

GIVING THE BREAD AND CUP
The bread and cup are given to the people, with these or other words being exchanged:
The body of Christ, given for you. **Amen.**
The blood of Christ, given for you. **Amen.**

PRAYER AFTER RECEIVING
Eternal God, we give you thanks for this holy mystery
     in which you have given yourself to us.
May all our actions
     be living examples
          of followers of Christ.
Grant that we may go into the world
     in the strength of your Spirit,
          to give ourselves for others.
in the name of Jesus Christ our Lord.
Amen.

Saint Luke [October 18]

Ecclesiasticus 38:1-4, 6-10; Psalm 147; 2 Timothy 4:5-13; Luke 4:14-21

The Lord be with you.
And also with you.
Lift up your hearts.
We lift them up to the Lord.
Let us give thanks to the Lord our God.
It is right to give our thanks and praise.

It is right, and a good and joyful thing
    always and everywhere to give thanks to you,
    Almighty God, Creator of heaven and earth.
To all who suffer
    you extend your healing hand
        through miracles,
        through the hands of physicians,
        and through medicines.

And so, with your people on earth
    and all the company of heaven,
    we praise your name and join their unending hymn:

Holy, holy, holy Lord, God of power and might,
heaven and earth are full of your glory.
    Hosanna in the highest.
Blessed is he who comes in the name of the Lord.
    Hosanna in the highest.

Holy are you, and blessed is your Son Jesus Christ.
    for he has fulfilled the scriptures.

Your Spirit anointed him
    to preach good news to the poor,
    to proclaim release to the captives and
    recovering of sight to the blind,
    to set at liberty those who are oppressed, and
    to announce that the time had come
    when you would save your people.
He healed the sick, fed the hungry, and ate with sinners.

By the baptism of his suffering, death, and resurrection,
    you gave birth to your church,
    delivered us from slavery to sin and death,
    and made with us a new covenant
    by water and the Spirit.

On the night in which he gave himself up for us
    he took bread, gave thanks to you, broke the bread,
    gave it to his disciples, and said,
"Take, eat; this is my body which is given for you.
Do this in remembrance of me."

When the supper was over he took the cup,
    gave thanks to you, gave it to his disciples, and said,
"Drink from this, all of you; this is my blood of the
    new covenant poured out for you and for many
        for the forgiveness of sins.
Do this as often as you drink it,
    in remembrance of me."

And so, in remembrance of these your mighty acts in Jesus Christ,
we offer ourselves in praise and thanksgiving
    as a holy and living sacrifice,
    in union with Christ's offering for us,
as we proclaim the mystery of faith.

Christ has died; Christ is risen; Christ will come again.

Pour out your Holy Spirit on us gathered here,
    and on these gifts of bread and wine.
Make them be for us the body and blood of Christ,
that we may be for the world the body of Christ,
    redeemed by his blood,
    that we might finish the race that is set before us.
Empower us to continue the work of evangelists and healers.

By your Spirit make us one with Christ,
    one with each other and
    one in ministry to all the world,
until Christ comes in final victory and
    we feast at the heavenly banquet.

Through your Son Jesus Christ,
with the Holy Spirit in your holy church,
all honor and glory is yours, almighty God,
    now and for ever.

Amen.

THE LORD'S PRAYER
And now with the confidence of children of God, let us pray: **Our Father...**

BREAKING THE BREAD
The pastor breaks the bread in silence, or while saying:
Because there is one loaf,
we, who are many, are one body, for we all partake of the one loaf.
The bread which we break is a sharing in the body of Christ.

The pastor lifts the cup in silence, or while saying:
The cup over which we give thanks is a sharing in the blood of Christ.

GIVING THE BREAD AND CUP
The bread and cup are given to the people, with these or other words being exchanged:
The body of Christ, given for you. **Amen.**
The blood of Christ, given for you. **Amen.**

PRAYER AFTER RECEIVING
Eternal God, we give you thanks for this holy mystery
    in which you have given yourself to us.
Help us lead in speech and conduct,
    in love, in faith, and in purity.
Grant that we may go into the world
    in the strength of your Spirit,
    to give ourselves for others.
in the name of Jesus Christ our Lord.
Amen.

Deuteronomy 34:1-12; Psalm 90:1-6, 13-17; 1 Thessalonians 2:1-8; Matthew 22:34-46

The Lord be with you.
And also with you.
Lift up your hearts.
We lift them up to the Lord.
Let us give thanks to the Lord our God.
It is right to give our thanks and praise.

It is right, and a good and joyful thing
    always and everywhere to give thanks to you,
    Almighty God, Creator of heaven and earth.
Lord, you have been our dwelling place in all generations.
Before the mountains were brought forth, or ever
    you formed the earth and the world;
from everlasting to everlasting
    you are God.

And so, with your people on earth
    and all the company of heaven,
    we praise your name and join their unending hymn:

Holy, holy, holy Lord, God of power and might,
heaven and earth are full of your glory.
    Hosanna in the highest.
Blessed is he who comes in the name of the Lord.
    Hosanna in the highest.

Holy are you, and blessed is your Son Jesus Christ.
He taught us that love
    is the greatest commandment of all.

Your Spirit anointed him
    to preach good news to the poor,
    to proclaim release to the captives and
    recovering of sight to the blind,
    to set at liberty those who are oppressed, and
    to announce that the time had come
    when you would save your people.
He healed the sick, fed the hungry, and ate with sinners.

By the baptism of his suffering, death, and resurrection,
 you gave birth to your church,
 delivered us from slavery to sin and death,
 and made with us a new covenant
 by water and the Spirit.

On the night in which he gave himself up for us
 he took bread, gave thanks to you, broke the bread,
 gave it to his disciples, and said,
"Take, eat; this is my body which is given for you.
Do this in remembrance of me."

When the supper was over he took the cup,
 gave thanks to you, gave it to his disciples, and said,
"Drink from this, all of you; this is my blood of the
 new covenant poured out for you and for many
 for the forgiveness of sins.
Do this as often as you drink it,
 in remembrance of me."

And so, in remembrance of these your mighty acts in Jesus Christ,
we offer ourselves in praise and thanksgiving
 as a holy and living sacrifice,
 in union with Christ's offering for us,
as we proclaim the mystery of faith.

Christ has died; Christ is risen; Christ will come again.

Pour out your Holy Spirit on us gathered here,
 and on these gifts of bread and wine.
Make them be for us the body and blood of Christ,
that we may be for the world the body of Christ,
 redeemed by his blood,
and infused with the spirit
 of love.

By your Spirit make us one with Christ,
 one with each other and
 one in ministry to all the world,
until Christ comes in final victory and
 we feast at the heavenly banquet.

Through your Son Jesus Christ,
with the Holy Spirit in your holy church,
all honor and glory is yours, almighty God,
   now and for ever.

Amen.

THE LORD'S PRAYER

And now with the confidence of children of God, let us pray: **Our Father...**

BREAKING THE BREAD

The pastor breaks the bread in silence, or while saying:
Because there is one loaf,
we, who are many, are one body, for we all partake of the one loaf.
The bread which we break is a sharing in the body of Christ.

The pastor lifts the cup in silence, or while saying:
The cup over which we give thanks is a sharing in the blood of Christ.

GIVING THE BREAD AND CUP

The bread and cup are given to the people, with these or other words being exchanged:
The body of Christ, given for you. **Amen.**
The blood of Christ, given for you. **Amen.**

PRAYER AFTER RECEIVING

Eternal God, we give you thanks for this holy mystery
   in which you have given yourself to us.
May love be
   the only way we live.
Grant that we may go into the world
   in the strength of your Spirit,
   to give ourselves for others.
in the name of Jesus Christ our Lord.
Amen.

Joshua 3:7-17; Psalm 107:1-7, 33-37; 1 Thessalonians 2:9-13; Matthew 23:1-12

The Lord be with you.
And also with you.
Lift up your hearts.
We lift them up to the Lord.
Let us give thanks to the Lord our God.
It is right to give our thanks and praise.

It is right, and a good and joyful thing
    always and everywhere to give thanks to you,
    Almighty God, Creator of heaven and earth.
We give thanks to you, O Lord, for you are good;
    your steadfast love endures forever.
You satisfy the thirsty
    and fill the hungry with good things.
You provide for all our needs.

And so, with your people on earth
    and all the company of heaven,
    we praise your name and join their unending hymn:

Holy, holy, holy Lord, God of power and might,
heaven and earth are full of your glory.
    Hosanna in the highest.
Blessed is he who comes in the name of the Lord.
    Hosanna in the highest.

Holy are you, and blessed is your Son Jesus Christ.
He showed that all who exalt themselves will be humbled
    and those who humble themselves will be exalted.

Your Spirit anointed him
    to preach good news to the poor,
    to proclaim release to the captives and
    recovering of sight to the blind,
    to set at liberty those who are oppressed, and
    to announce that the time had come
    when you would save your people.
He healed the sick, fed the hungry, and ate with sinners.

By the baptism of his suffering, death, and resurrection,
    you gave birth to your church,
    delivered us from slavery to sin and death,
    and made with us a new covenant
    by water and the Spirit.

On the night in which he gave himself up for us
    he took bread, gave thanks to you, broke the bread,
    gave it to his disciples, and said,
"Take, eat; this is my body which is given for you.
Do this in remembrance of me."

When the supper was over he took the cup,
    gave thanks to you, gave it to his disciples, and said,
"Drink from this, all of you; this is my blood of the
    new covenant poured out for you and for many
        for the forgiveness of sins.
Do this as often as you drink it,
    in remembrance of me."

And so, in remembrance of these your mighty acts in Jesus Christ,
we offer ourselves in praise and thanksgiving
    as a holy and living sacrifice,
    in union with Christ's offering for us,
as we proclaim the mystery of faith.

Christ has died; Christ is risen; Christ will come again.

Pour out your Holy Spirit on us gathered here,
    and on these gifts of bread and wine.
Make them be for us the body and blood of Christ,
that we may be for the world the body of Christ,
    redeemed by his blood,
for we are his witnesses
    to an unbelieving world.

By your Spirit make us one with Christ,
    one with each other and
    one in ministry to all the world,
until Christ comes in final victory and
    we feast at the heavenly banquet.

Through your Son Jesus Christ,
with the Holy Spirit in your holy church,
all honor and glory is yours, almighty God,
   now and for ever.

Amen.

The Lord's Prayer

And now with the confidence of children of God, let us pray: **Our Father...**

Breaking the Bread

The pastor breaks the bread in silence, or while saying:
Because there is one loaf,
we, who are many, are one body, for we all partake of the one loaf.
The bread which we break is a sharing in the body of Christ.

The pastor lifts the cup in silence, or while saying:
The cup over which we give thanks is a sharing in the blood of Christ.

Giving the Bread and Cup

The bread and cup are given to the people, with these or other words being exchanged:
The body of Christ, given for you. **Amen.**
The blood of Christ, given for you. **Amen.**

Prayer after Receiving

Eternal God, we give you thanks for this holy mystery
   in which you have given yourself to us.
May our every act
   be a thanksgiving to you.
Grant that we may go into the world
      in the strength of your Spirit,
      to give ourselves for others.
in the name of Jesus Christ our Lord.
Amen.

Revelation 7:9-17; Psalm 34:1-10, 22; 1 John 3:1-3; Matthew 5:1-12

The Lord be with you.
And also with you.
Lift up your hearts.
We lift them up to the Lord.
Let us give thanks to the Lord our God.
It is right to give our thanks and praise.

It is right, and a good and joyful thing
    always and everywhere to give thanks to you,
    Almighty God, Creator of heaven and earth.
The heavenly multitude proclaims:
Salvation belongs to you,
    O God seated on your throne
        and to the Lamb!
Blessing and glory and wisdom and thanksgiving
    and honor and power and might
        be to You forever and ever.

And so, with your people on earth
and all the company of heaven,
      [including: *pause here for members of the congregation to name out loud*
      persons who have died...
        ...and those whom we name in our hearts,]
  we praise your name and join their unending hymn:

Holy, holy, holy Lord, God of power and might,
heaven and earth are full of your glory.
    Hosanna in the highest.
Blessed is he who comes in the name of the Lord.
    Hosanna in the highest.

Holy are you, and blessed is your Son Jesus Christ.
Through him we are your beloved children.
What we will be
    has not yet been revealed.
When Christ is revealed,
    we will be like him,
        for we will see him as he is.

Your Spirit anointed him
    to preach good news to the poor,
    to proclaim release to the captives and
    recovering of sight to the blind,
    to set at liberty those who are oppressed, and
    to announce that the time had come
    when you would save your people.
He healed the sick, fed the hungry, and ate with sinners.

By the baptism of his suffering, death, and resurrection,
    you gave birth to your church,
    delivered us from slavery to sin and death,
    and made with us a new covenant
    by water and the Spirit.

On the night in which he gave himself up for us
    he took bread, gave thanks to you, broke the bread,
    gave it to his disciples, and said,
"Take, eat; this is my body which is given for you.
Do this in remembrance of me."

When the supper was over he took the cup,
    gave thanks to you, gave it to his disciples, and said,
"Drink from this, all of you; this is my blood of the
    new covenant poured out for you and for many
        for the forgiveness of sins.
Do this as often as you drink it,
    in remembrance of me."

And so, in remembrance of these your mighty acts in Jesus Christ,
we offer ourselves in praise and thanksgiving
    as a holy and living sacrifice,
    in union with Christ's offering for us,
as we proclaim the mystery of faith.

Christ has died; Christ is risen; Christ will come again.

Pour out your Holy Spirit on us gathered here,
    and on these gifts of bread and wine.
Make them be for us the body and blood of Christ,
that we may be for the world the body of Christ,
    redeemed by his blood,
for we live in hope
    of what is yet to be revealed.

By your Spirit make us one with Christ,
    one with each other and
    one in ministry to all the world,
until Christ comes in final victory and
    we feast at the heavenly banquet.

Through your Son Jesus Christ,
with the Holy Spirit in your holy church,
all honor and glory is yours, almighty God,
    now and for ever.

Amen.

THE LORD'S PRAYER
And now with the confidence of children of God, let us pray: **Our Father...**

BREAKING THE BREAD
The pastor breaks the bread in silence, or while saying:
Because there is one loaf,
we, who are many, are one body, for we all partake of the one loaf.
The bread which we break is a sharing in the body of Christ.

The pastor lifts the cup in silence, or while saying:
The cup over which we give thanks is a sharing in the blood of Christ.

GIVING THE BREAD AND CUP
The bread and cup are given to the people, with these or other words being exchanged:
The body of Christ, given for you. **Amen.**
The blood of Christ, given for you. **Amen.**

Eternal God, we give you thanks for this holy mystery
 in which you have given yourself to us.
We pray that we may follow
 the exampleof the saints
as we live our lives
 in faith and hope.
Grant that we may go into the world
 in the strength of your Spirit,
 to give ourselves for others.
in the name of Jesus Christ our Lord.
Amen.

Joshua 24:1-3a, 14-25; Psalm 78:1-7; 1 Thessalonians 4:13-18; Matthew 25:1-13

The Lord be with you.
And also with you.
Lift up your hearts.
We lift them up to the Lord.
Let us give thanks to the Lord our God.
It is right to give our thanks and praise.

It is right, and a good and joyful thing
    always and everywhere to give thanks to you,
    Almighty God, Creator of heaven and earth.
You delivered your people
    from slavery to freedom
and made covenant with them
    that you would be their God
        and they would be your people.

And so, with your people on earth
    and all the company of heaven,
    we praise your name and join their unending hymn:

Holy, holy, holy Lord, God of power and might,
heaven and earth are full of your glory.
    Hosanna in the highest.
Blessed is he who comes in the name of the Lord.
    Hosanna in the highest.

Holy are you, and blessed is your Son Jesus Christ.
He showed us the way to you,
    that we not put anything above you.

Your Spirit anointed him
    to preach good news to the poor,
    to proclaim release to the captives and
    recovering of sight to the blind,
    to set at liberty those who are oppressed, and
    to announce that the time had come
    when you would save your people.
He healed the sick, fed the hungry, and ate with sinners.

By the baptism of his suffering, death, and resurrection,
    you gave birth to your church,
    delivered us from slavery to sin and death,
    and made with us a new covenant
    by water and the Spirit.

On the night in which he gave himself up for us
    he took bread, gave thanks to you, broke the bread,
    gave it to his disciples, and said,
"Take, eat; this is my body which is given for you.
Do this in remembrance of me."

When the supper was over he took the cup,
    gave thanks to you, gave it to his disciples, and said,
"Drink from this, all of you; this is my blood of the
    new covenant poured out for you and for many
        for the forgiveness of sins.
Do this as often as you drink it,
    in remembrance of me."

And so, in remembrance of these your mighty acts in Jesus Christ,
we offer ourselves in praise and thanksgiving
    as a holy and living sacrifice,
    in union with Christ's offering for us,
as we proclaim the mystery of faith.

Christ has died; Christ is risen; Christ will come again.

Pour out your Holy Spirit on us gathered here,
    and on these gifts of bread and wine.
Make them be for us the body and blood of Christ,
that we may be for the world the body of Christ,
    redeemed by his blood,
that we might always be ready
    when called.

By your Spirit make us one with Christ,
    one with each other and
    one in ministry to all the world,
until Christ comes in final victory and
    we feast at the heavenly banquet.

Through your Son Jesus Christ,
with the Holy Spirit in your holy church,
all honor and glory is yours, almighty God,
    now and for ever.

Amen.

THE LORD'S PRAYER

And now with the confidence of children of God, let us pray: **Our Father...**

BREAKING THE BREAD

The pastor breaks the bread in silence, or while saying:
Because there is one loaf,
we, who are many, are one body, for we all partake of the one loaf.
The bread which we break is a sharing in the body of Christ.

The pastor lifts the cup in silence, or while saying:
The cup over which we give thanks is a sharing in the blood of Christ.

GIVING THE BREAD AND CUP

The bread and cup are given to the people, with these or other words being exchanged:
The body of Christ, given for you. **Amen.**
The blood of Christ, given for you. **Amen.**

PRAYER AFTER RECEIVING

Eternal God, we give you thanks for this holy mystery
    in which you have given yourself to us.
We hereby forsake
    the false gods of our society
        and pledge to live only to you.
Grant that we may go into the world
    in the strength of your Spirit,
        to give ourselves for others.
in the name of Jesus Christ our Lord.
Amen.

Judges 4:1-7; Psalm 123 or Psalm 76; 1 Thessalonians 5:1-11; Matthew 25:14-30

The Lord be with you.
And also with you.
Lift up your hearts.
We lift them up to the Lord.
Let us give thanks to the Lord our God.
It is right to give our thanks and praise.

It is right, and a good and joyful thing
    always and everywhere to give thanks to you,
      Almighty God, Creator of heaven and earth.
When your people did what was evil
    you put them into the hands of their enemy.
But then you offered to save them
    through your judge Deborah.

And so, with your people on earth
    and all the company of heaven,
    we praise your name and join their unending hymn:

Holy, holy, holy Lord, God of power and might,
heaven and earth are full of your glory.
    Hosanna in the highest.
Blessed is he who comes in the name of the Lord.
    Hosanna in the highest.

Holy are you, and blessed is your Son Jesus Christ.
He is the Lord of the living and the dead,
    for all who believe in him
      shall have eternal life.

Your Spirit anointed him
    to preach good news to the poor,
    to proclaim release to the captives and
    recovering of sight to the blind,
    to set at liberty those who are oppressed, and
    to announce that the time had come
    when you would save your people.
He healed the sick, fed the hungry, and ate with sinners.

By the baptism of his suffering, death, and resurrection,
    you gave birth to your church,
    delivered us from slavery to sin and death,
    and made with us a new covenant
    by water and the Spirit.

On the night in which he gave himself up for us
    he took bread, gave thanks to you, broke the bread,
    gave it to his disciples, and said,
"Take, eat; this is my body which is given for you.
Do this in remembrance of me."

When the supper was over he took the cup,
    gave thanks to you, gave it to his disciples, and said,
"Drink from this, all of you; this is my blood of the
    new covenant poured out for you and for many
        for the forgiveness of sins.
Do this as often as you drink it,
    in remembrance of me."

And so, in remembrance of these your mighty acts in Jesus Christ,
we offer ourselves in praise and thanksgiving
    as a holy and living sacrifice,
    in union with Christ's offering for us,
as we proclaim the mystery of faith.

Christ has died; Christ is risen; Christ will come again.

Pour out your Holy Spirit on us gathered here,
    and on these gifts of bread and wine.
Make them be for us the body and blood of Christ,
that we may be for the world the body of Christ,
    redeemed by his blood,
that we might be called
    children of the light.

By your Spirit make us one with Christ,
    one with each other and
    one in ministry to all the world,
until Christ comes in final victory and
    we feast at the heavenly banquet.

Through your Son Jesus Christ,
with the Holy Spirit in your holy church,
all honor and glory is yours, almighty God,
    now and for ever.

Amen.

THE LORD'S PRAYER

And now with the confidence of children of God, let us pray: **Our Father...**

BREAKING THE BREAD

The pastor breaks the bread in silence, or while saying:
Because there is one loaf,
we, who are many, are one body, for we all partake of the one loaf.
The bread which we break is a sharing in the body of Christ.

The pastor lifts the cup in silence, or while saying:
The cup over which we give thanks is a sharing in the blood of Christ.

GIVING THE BREAD AND CUP

The bread and cup are given to the people, with these or other words being exchanged:
The body of Christ, given for you. **Amen.**
The blood of Christ, given for you. **Amen.**

PRAYER AFTER RECEIVING

Eternal God, we give you thanks for this holy mystery
    in which you have given yourself to us.
As children of the light,
    we pledge to use our gifts and talents
        to help usher in your kingdom
            here on earth.
Grant that we may go into the world
    in the strength of your Spirit,
    to give ourselves for others.
in the name of Jesus Christ our Lord.
Amen.

Christ the King (The Reign of Christ) [November 20-26] (a)

Ezekiel 34:11-16, 20-24; Psalm 100; Ephesians 1:15-23; Matthew 25:31-46

The Lord be with you.
And also with you.
Lift up your hearts.
We lift them up to the Lord.
Let us give thanks to the Lord our God.
It is right to give our thanks and praise.

It is right, and a good and joyful thing
    always and everywhere to give thanks to you,
    Almighty God, Creator of heaven and earth.
We are yours:
    your people and the sheep of your pasture.
Let us enter your gates with thanksgiving,
    and your courts with praise;
for you are good and your steadfast love endures forever.

And so, with your people on earth
    and all the company of heaven,
    we praise your name and join their unending hymn:

Holy, holy, holy Lord, God of power and might,
heaven and earth are full of your glory.
    Hosanna in the highest.
Blessed is he who comes in the name of the Lord.
    Hosanna in the highest.

Holy are you, and blessed is your Son Jesus Christ.
You put his power to work when you raised him from the dead
    and seated him at your right hand.

Your Spirit anointed him
    to preach good news to the poor,
    to proclaim release to the captives and
    recovering of sight to the blind,
    to set at liberty those who are oppressed, and
    to announce that the time had come
    when you would save your people.
He healed the sick, fed the hungry, and ate with sinners.

By the baptism of his suffering, death, and resurrection,
   you gave birth to your church,
   delivered us from slavery to sin and death,
   and made with us a new covenant
   by water and the Spirit.

On the night in which he gave himself up for us
   he took bread, gave thanks to you, broke the bread,
   gave it to his disciples, and said,
"Take, eat; this is my body which is given for you.
Do this in remembrance of me."

When the supper was over he took the cup,
   gave thanks to you, gave it to his disciples, and said,
"Drink from this, all of you; this is my blood of the
   new covenant poured out for you and for many
      for the forgiveness of sins.
Do this as often as you drink it,
   in remembrance of me."

And so, in remembrance of these your mighty acts in Jesus Christ,
we offer ourselves in praise and thanksgiving
   as a holy and living sacrifice,
   in union with Christ's offering for us,
as we proclaim the mystery of faith.

Christ has died; Christ is risen; Christ will come again.

Pour out your Holy Spirit on us gathered here,
   and on these gifts of bread and wine.
Make them be for us the body and blood of Christ,
that we may be for the world the body of Christ,
   redeemed by his blood.
Through it we celebrate his reign in our lives
   and throughout all the lands.

By your Spirit make us one with Christ,
   one with each other and
   one in ministry to all the world,
until Christ comes in final victory and
   we feast at the heavenly banquet.

Through your Son Jesus Christ,
with the Holy Spirit in your holy church,
all honor and glory is yours, almighty God,
   now and for ever.

Amen.

THE LORD'S PRAYER

And now with the confidence of children of God, let us pray: **Our Father...**

BREAKING THE BREAD

The pastor breaks the bread in silence, or while saying:
Because there is one loaf,
we, who are many, are one body, for we all partake of the one loaf.
The bread which we break is a sharing in the body of Christ.

The pastor lifts the cup in silence, or while saying:
The cup over which we give thanks is a sharing in the blood of Christ.

GIVING THE BREAD AND CUP

The bread and cup are given to the people, with these or other words being exchanged:
The body of Christ, given for you. **Amen.**
The blood of Christ, given for you. **Amen.**

PRAYER AFTER RECEIVING

Eternal God, we give you thanks for this holy mystery
   in which you have given yourself to us.
Empower us
   to see your presence
      even in the least likely places.
Grant that we may go into the world
   in the strength of your Spirit,
   to give ourselves for others.
in the name of Jesus Christ our Lord.
Amen.

Thanksgiving Day (a)

Deuteronomy 8:7-18; Psalm 65; 2 Corinthians 9:6-15; Luke 17:11-19

The Lord be with you.
And also with you.
Lift up your hearts.
We lift them up to the Lord.
Let us give thanks to the Lord our God.
It is right to give our thanks and praise.

It is right, and a good and joyful thing
  always and everywhere to give thanks to you,
    Almighty God, Creator of heaven and earth.
You set the stars in the skies
  and the planets spinning around them.
You handiwork is too wondrous
  for mere mortals to comprehend.
We marvel at your great works.

And so, with your people on earth
  and all the company of heaven,
    we praise your name and join their unending hymn:

Holy, holy, holy Lord, God of power and might,
heaven and earth are full of your glory.
  Hosanna in the highest.
Blessed is he who comes in the name of the Lord.
  Hosanna in the highest.

Holy are you, and blessed is your Son Jesus Christ.
He demonstrated your generous love
  and showed us how to thank you.

Your Spirit anointed him
  to preach good news to the poor,
  to proclaim release to the captives and
  recovering of sight to the blind,
  to set at liberty those who are oppressed, and
  to announce that the time had come
  when you would save your people.
He healed the sick, fed the hungry, and ate with sinners.

218

O'Donnell, Lift Up Your Hearts 3rd ed. Year A

By the baptism of his suffering, death, and resurrection,
   you gave birth to your church,
   delivered us from slavery to sin and death,
   and made with us a new covenant
   by water and the Spirit.

On the night in which he gave himself up for us
   he took bread, gave thanks to you, broke the bread,
   gave it to his disciples, and said,
"Take, eat; this is my body which is given for you.
Do this in remembrance of me."

When the supper was over he took the cup,
   gave thanks to you, gave it to his disciples, and said,
"Drink from this, all of you; this is my blood of the
   new covenant poured out for you and for many
      for the forgiveness of sins.
Do this as often as you drink it,
   in remembrance of me."

And so, in remembrance of these your mighty acts in Jesus Christ,
we offer ourselves in praise and thanksgiving
   as a holy and living sacrifice,
   in union with Christ's offering for us,
as we proclaim the mystery of faith.

Christ has died; Christ is risen; Christ will come again.

Pour out your Holy Spirit on us gathered here,
   and on these gifts of bread and wine.
Make them be for us the body and blood of Christ,
that we may be for the world the body of Christ,
   redeemed by his blood.
May we treat your creation
   with honor and respect.

By your Spirit make us one with Christ,
   one with each other and
   one in ministry to all the world,
until Christ comes in final victory and
   we feast at the heavenly banquet.

Through your Son Jesus Christ,
with the Holy Spirit in your holy church,
all honor and glory is yours, almighty God,
    now and for ever.

Amen.

THE LORD'S PRAYER

And now with the confidence of children of God, let us pray: **Our Father...**

BREAKING THE BREAD

The pastor breaks the bread in silence, or while saying:
Because there is one loaf,
we, who are many, are one body, for we all partake of the one loaf.
The bread which we break is a sharing in the body of Christ.

The pastor lifts the cup in silence, or while saying:
The cup over which we give thanks is a sharing in the blood of Christ.

GIVING THE BREAD AND CUP

The bread and cup are given to the people, with these or other words being exchanged:
The body of Christ, given for you. **Amen.**
The blood of Christ, given for you. **Amen.**

PRAYER AFTER RECEIVING

Eternal God, we give you thanks for this holy mystery
    in which you have given yourself to us.
We rejoice in all you have given us.
Grant that we may go into the world
    in the strength of your Spirit,
        to give ourselves for others.
in the name of Jesus Christ our Lord.
Amen.

See also the UNITED METHODIST BOOK OF WORSHIP, 559-567.

Now may our Lord Jesus Christ himself and God our Father,
    who loved us and through grace gave us eternal comfort and good hope,
    comfort your hearts and strengthen them in every good work and word.
Amen.

from 2 Thessalonians 2:16-17 (Nov 6-12)

Finally, beloved,
    whatever is true, whatever is honorable, whatever is just,
    whatever is pure, whatever is pleasing, whatever is commendable,
    if there is any excellence and if there is anything worthy of praise,
think about these things.
Keep on doing the things
    that you have learned and received and heard and seen here,
and the God of peace will be with you.
Amen.

from Philippians 4:8-9

Rejoice in the Lord always; again I will say, Rejoice.
Let your gentleness be known to everyone. The Lord is near.
Do not worry about anything,
    but in everything by prayer and supplication with thanksgiving,
    let your requests be made known to God.
And the peace of God, which surpasses all understanding,
    will guard your hearts and your minds in Christ Jesus.
Amen.

from Philippians 4:4-7

The grace of the Lord Jesus Christ
    and the love of God
    and the fellowship of the Holy Spirit
    be with you now and forever.
Amen.

from 2 Corinthians 13:14

The Lord bless you and keep you:
The Lord's face shine upon you and be gracious to you:
The Lord lift up the Divine countenance upon you
    and give you peace.
    Amen.   *from Numbers 6:24:26*

Now may the God of peace
    who brought again from the dead
        our Lord Jesus Christ,
           who is the great Shepherd of the sheep,
by the blood of the eternal covenant,
    equip you with every good thing
that you may do the divine will,
    doing everything that is pleasing to God.
To Jesus Christ be the glory for ever.
Amen.

from Hebrews 13:20-21

May the peace of God
    which passes all understanding,
keep your hearts and minds
    in the knowledge and love of God,
    and of the Savior Jesus Christ our Lord;
And the blessing of Almighty God,
    the blessed and holy Trinity,
    be with you always.
Amen.

To the blessed and only Sovereign,
    the Ruler of rulers and Lord of lords,
        who alone has immortality
        and who dwells in unapproachable light,
    whom no one has ever seen or can see:
Be honor and eternal glory.
Amen.

from 1 Timothy 6:15-16

Now to the one who
    by the power at work within us
is able to do far more than we can ask or think:
Be glory in the Church
    and in Christ Jesus
to all generations for ever.
Amen.

from Ephesians 3:20-21

The God of all grace,
    who has called you to divine glory by Christ,
will restore, establish, and strengthen you.
To God be the glory now and for ever.
Amen.

from 1 Peter 5:10-11

May the God of hope
    fill you with all joy and peace in believing,
so that you may abound in hope
    by the power of the Holy Spirit.
Amen.

from Romans 15:13

May the God of steadfastness and encouragement
grant you to live in such harmony with one another,
    in accord with Jesus Christ,
that you may with one voice glorify God.
Amen.

from Romans 15:5

Be patient, brothers and sisters, until the coming of the Lord.
Be patient. Strengthen your hearts, for the coming of the Lord is near.
Do not grumble against one another, so that you may not be judged.
See, the judge is standing at the doors.
Go forth in joy in the name of the Father, Son, and Holy Spirit.
Amen.

from James 5:7-9

The Spirit of the Lord is upon you.
Go forth and do justice.
Love kindness.
Always walk humbly with God.
In the name of the Father, Son, and Holy Spirit.
Amen.

from Micah 6:8

Ecumenical Text

Our Father in heaven,
  hallowed be your name,
  your kingdom come,
  your will be done, on earth as in heaven.
Give us today our daily bread.
Forgive us our sins
  as we forgive those who sin against us.
Save us from the time of trial
  and deliver us from evil.
For the kingdom, the power, and the glory are yours,
  now and for ever. **Amen.**

Traditional Text (former Methodist Church)

Our Father, who art in heaven,
  hallowed be thy Name,
  thy kingdom come,
  thy will be done on earth as it is in heaven.
Give us this day our daily bread.
And forgive us our trespasses,
  as we forgive those who trespass against us.
And lead us not into temptation,
  but deliver us from evil.
For thine is the kingdom, and the power, and the glory, forever. **Amen.**

Traditional Text (former Evangelical United Brethren Church)

Our Father, who art in heaven,
  hallowed be thy name;
  thy kingdom come,
  thy will be done, on earth as it is in heaven.
Give us this day our daily bread;
and forgive us our debts,
  as we forgive our debtors;
and lead us not into temptation,
  but deliver us from evil.
For thine is the kingdom and the power and the glory, forever. **Amen.**

Made in the USA
Las Vegas, NV
04 December 2021